2. 20-74

Soviet International Trade
in Heckscher-Ohlin
Perspective

Soviet International Trade in Heckscher-Ohlin Perspective

An Input-Output Study

Steven Rosefielde
University of North Carolina

Lexington Books
D.C. Heath and Company
Lexington, Massachusetts
Toronto   London

Library of Congress Cataloging in Publication Data

Rosefielde, Steven.
    Soviet international trade in Heckscher-Ohlin perspective.

    Bibliography: p.
    1. Russia—Commerce. 2. Interindustry economics. 3. Russia—Com-
merce—Mathematical models I. Title.
HF3626.5.R68   382'.0947   73-6851
ISBN 0-669-87098-6

Published simultaneously in Canada.

Printed in the United States of America.

International Standard Book Number: 0-669-87098-6

Library of Congress Catalog Card Number: 73:6851

To Susan

"Be in me as the eternal moods of bleak winds, and not as transient things are, gaiety and flowers, . . ." (Ezra Pound).

[793091]

Contents

List of Figures

List of Tables

Preface

This study seeks to assess the economic rationality of Soviet foreign trade from the standpoint of modern economic theory. The approach is a novel one in the context of the Soviet economy, although it has been widely applied in the study of market economies. Specifically, we employ as our theoretical standard the Heckscher-Ohlin theorem which maintains that the fundamental determinant of the opportunity costs governing the commodity structure of foreign trade is relative international factor availabilities. The opportunity to apply Heckscher-Ohlin theory to the Soviet economy has only recently become a reality with the publication of the 1959 Soviet input-output table, together with coefficients for converting import and export statistics from foreign trade ruble to domestic wholesale producers' prices. Following the methodology first laid out by Wassily Leontief's pioneering work on U.S. factor proportions in 1953,* we calculate factor proportions generated in Soviet trade with the world as a whole, and extending this basic method we also compute bilateral factor proportion statistics for Soviet trade with individual countries as well as with three well-defined political entities, the CMEA, developed western nations, and a group of less developed countries.

Since the literature on empirical tests of the Heckscher-Ohlin theory in an input-output format has grown quite extensive in recent years, centering on the question of the influence of third factors on the Leontief calculation of U.S. factor proportions, we examine the more important of these hypotheses, particularly the influence of natural resources and skilled labor-cum-technology in order to assess their significance in the Soviet context. This approach is supplemented by an investigation of trends in the commodity composition of Soviet traded goods to obtain deeper insight into the causal nexus governing the Soviet trade decision process.

As the reader will discover, Soviet international trade turns out to be highly Heckscher-Ohlin rational, especially in comparison with analogous American findings. An extended inquiry into the causes of this paradoxical situation is therefore undertaken in the concluding chapters which shows the overall rationality of Soviet foreign trade planning in a favorable light.

The book is divided into four parts: a review of Heckscher-Ohlin theory, coupled with a description of data sources and computational procedures (Chapters 1-3); a study of Soviet factor proportions (Chapters 4-6); an analysis of the relationship between trends in the commodity composition of Soviet traded goods and trends in Soviet factor proportions statistics (Chapter 7), and an assessment of the relationship between the Soviet foreign trade decision

---

*Wassily Leontief, "Domestic Production and Foreign Trade: The American Capital Position Re-examined," PROCEEDINGS OF THE AMERICAN PHILOSOPHICAL SOCIETY, Sept. 1953, 97, 332-49.

making process and our empirical findings (Chapter 8). A review of the basic results of the study along with some summary conclusions appear in Chapter 9.

Although this book has been written primarily for professional economists, its contents should be of vital interest to political scientists, economic sociologists, students of Soviet affairs and the business community at large concerned with a deeper comprehension of the foreign trade behavior of an archetypal centrally planned, socialist economy. For non-economists Chapters 2, 3 and 5 can be omitted without serious loss.

Acknowledgments

The author would like to acknowledge his gratitude for the guidance and encouragement of Professors Abram Bergson and Anne Carter without which this book could not have been written.

Professors Vladimir G. Treml, J.M. Montias, Franklyn Holzman, Martin and Dina Spechler have all, in one way or another, assisted me by clarifying various difficulties and ambiguities in the text. Diane Deaton stoically typed and retyped seemingly endless versions of the manuscript. To all of the above the author wishes to express his profound appreciation. In acknowledging his debt to others, however, the author of course in no way holds them responsible for any errors that may remain.

The author also wishes to thank the Ford Foundation for its support. Much of the theoretical research underlying Chapter 8 was developed under the auspices of a joint UNC-DUKE Ford Foundation grant for the study of the Soviet economy in input-output perspective.

Last but not least, I would like to thank my gracious wife for her assistance in ways too numerous to describe.

**Part I
Soviet Factor Proportions:
Problems of Theory, Data,
and Computation**

1

The Role of Factor Proportions in International Trade: Problems of Theory and Measurement

The impact of international trade on domestic factor structure has long been a politically and economically significant subject. The work of Heckscher and Ohlin, along with modern extensions by Samuelson and others, proves the durability of the interest in this topic. A key facet of the modern approach to the study of factors in an international trade context has been the emphasis on factor proportions as opposed to factor flows. It is our intention to follow in the footsteps of the Heckscher-Ohlin school in our analysis of the role of domestic Soviet factors in Soviet international trade, but it should be noted that this choice requires some justification since logically when gains from trade are considered one normally thinks in terms of net advantage, rather than of commodity or factor proportions. The precise nature of the theoretical superiority of the factor proportions approach can only be brought out by contrasting the advantages and disadvantages of these alternative modes of analysis. We will therefore set forth the conceptual framework of the factor proportions and net factor flow methods in the next few pages, and at the same time will point out some of the more subtle computational aspects of the factor proportions approach frequently overlooked.

A. Net Factor Flows

Suppose we could partition economic variables into two classes, inputs and outputs. Let us call the input class factors and assume that there exist m such factors x_i, $i = i\,(1, \ldots, m)$. Assume in addition that factors are freely mobile and can be statistically classified in the national income and labor migration accounts of some arbitrarily chosen country as imports or exports. Then for any given factor x_j we can describe its net factor flow simply as

$$\phi_j = x_j^e - x_j^m \tag{1.1}$$

where the superscript e = exports and m = imports.

Next suppose we desired to construct a summary measure of total net factor flow $\sum_{i=1}^{m} \phi_j$. In general, x_i and x_j will be measured in different units, so that some weighting system is required for aggregation. If markets are reasonably effective,

3

they will generate a general equilibrium set of factor prices π_i, $i = i(1, \ldots, m)$ which can be used as theoretically appropriate weights for the computation of total net factor flows

$$\phi = \sum_{i=1}^{m} \pi_i (x_i^e - x_i^m) \qquad (1.2)$$

Clearly if factors are homogenous, and prices rational, the calculation of net factor flows is a mere matter of acounting. Its economic significance will depend on particular applications. For example, an economist by using an aggregate production function could compute the increase or decrease in production potential afforded the society by its net factor flows.[1] If a net factor flow surplus occurs he could compare this magnitude with the foregone opportunities required in the commodity space to achieve this gain. Or in the spirit of Heckscher-Ohlin he could investigate the pattern of factor flows to assess whether the domestically scarce or the domestically abundant factor was being imported on balance, with its attendant impact on domestic factor proportions. Thus the net factor flow concept is not without its charm. Unfortunately, the factor flow computation outlined above has serious practical debilities. First and foremost, with the close of the nineteenth century the free international mobility of labor came to a halt. By any standard labor is a factor of the highest importance, so that its immobility greatly limits the usefulness of a net factor flow study. But this is not all. Land, except in the form of raw materials is necessarily fixed in situ, while capital, the other great neoclassical factor, has also found its mobility sharply curtailed since 1914.[2] Thus, the free mobility of factors cannot presently be considered essential to the international adjustment process to any important extent.

B. Net Embodied Factor Flows

If direct factor flows are restricted, the general equilibrium model of analysis would suggest that these constraints would be reflected in adjustments elsewhere in the system. In particular, the embodied factor structure of imports and exports might reflect factor exchange opportunities inherent in the international pattern of factor availabilities. Thus, if a given country vis-à-vis the world as a whole had an abundant supply of labor and a scarce supply of capital, a tendency for labor intensive exports and capital intensive imports might be anticipated since the scarce factor intensive goods in all likelihood would be less expensive abroad, while the labor intensive goods would be relatively cheap domestically. Such a notion is appealing, suggestive, and potentially misleading. Suppose we set out to make a net embodied factor flow study along the line of the net factor flow study just discussed. Proceeding as before, we would first calculate the net embodied factor flow content of traded goods for some representative factor x. Equation (1.3) tells us that the net embodied factor content of q_i is:

$$\hat{\phi} = \sum_{i=1}^{n} \alpha_i q_i^e - \beta_i q_i^m \qquad (1.3)$$

where: $\qquad \alpha_i = x_j^d / q_i \qquad\qquad\qquad i = i\ (1, \ldots, n)$

$\qquad\qquad \beta_i = x_j^f / q_i \qquad\qquad\qquad j = j\ (1, \ldots, m)$

Flows of factor x_j depend on the factor intensity x_j^d in all domestic production of q_i, x_j^d / q_i, and the factor intensity of x_j^f in all foreign production of q_i both multiplied by their respective total output of traded goods q_i. The magnitude $\hat{\phi}$ expresses the actual embodied net transfer of some homogenously defined factor.

Suppose we also desired to compute an aggregate of factors, say several labor skills, or total net embodied factor flows. Just as before we would need a set of weights with which to aggregate the heterogeneous mix of factors under consideration.

$$\hat{\phi} = \sum_{j=1}^{m} \sum_{i=1}^{n} \omega_j \alpha_i q_i^e - \nu_j \beta_i q_i^m \qquad \begin{array}{l} j = j\ (1, \ldots, m) \\ i = i\ (1, \ldots, n) \end{array} \qquad (1.4)$$

where:

$\qquad \omega_j \quad =$ the value weight of the x_jth factor embodied in the ith export good

$\qquad \nu_j \quad =$ the value weight of the x_jth factor embodied in the ith import good α_i

$\qquad \beta_i$ as defined in Equation (1.3)

Superficially Equation (1.4) appears to be a close analogue of Equation (1.2). The primary difference between these formulations being that one set of weights π_i's are used in Equation (1.2), while two sets of price weights ω_j's and ν_j's are employed in Equation (1.4). This distinction, however, is of crucial theoretical importance. The need for two price weight sets arises from the fact that marginal rates of factor substitution will generally differ from country to country. Only in the unrealistic case where production functions are identical, homogeneous of the first degree, with factors combined in the same proportions in all countries will $\omega_j = \nu_j$. When we considered direct net factor flows this difficulty did not arise because net factor imports could be valued in domestic market prices reflecting their internal market productivities. But if we tried to extend this procedure to embodied factor flows we would encounter the crucial theoretical complication that embodied factors cannot be disembodied at the port of disembarkation. Since commodities cannot be reconverted into their factor components, embodied factors cannot be substituted directly in production for normal domestic factor inputs, and therefore cannot legitimately be valued at the domestic rate of factor substitution. This means that Equation (1.4) will necessarily yield a theoretically ambiguous measure of net embodied factor flows. Suppose, as in this study, the ultimate objective of factor flow analysis was an assessment of the rationality of a country's international exchange given factor immobility amongst nations. Our measure of surrogate factor flows in embodied form would depend awkwardly on two marginal rates of technical factor substitution, the meaning of which would be open to dispute.

One possible way around this impasse would be to overlook the difficulty that disembodied factors and factors are incommensurable, by weighting both import and export intensities by the same coefficients $\omega_j, j = j\,(1, \ldots, m)$. The rationale for such a procedure lies in an argument invoking the commodity space. If the imported commodities were suddenly to be replaced by import competing substitutes, the domestic factors required for their production would be employed at prices reflecting the domestic economy-wide marginal rate of factor substitution. Of course, factor intensity ratios would still be different in the two economies, but if this is overlooked and domestic factor prices are used to weight embodied foreign factors, we would obtain a quasi-opportunity cost measure of net embodied factor transfers. This solution is unsatisfactory because it still implies that foreign factors are available as inputs into the domestic production function in proportions other than those prevailing domestically, but it will serve us well as a foil to bring out the inner rationality of the Leontief Statistic, which is the correct empirical formulation of the Heckscher-Ohlin approach and provides the proper theoretical resolution to the embodied factor flow problem.

C. Heckscher-Ohlin Factor Proportions Analysis

The Heckscher-Ohlin approach asserts that a given nation's comparative advantage is determined by the relative scarcity of *domestic factors*, so that imports should intensively embody the scarce domestic factor, and exports the abundant domestic factor. Note that the emphasis is on domestic factor proportions, and not the flow of embodied factors. From the viewpoint of any single country, it matters not at all what the actual factor content of its imports are; that is, for any aggregate neoclassical factor X_k

$$X_k = \sum_{i=1}^{n} v_k \beta_i q_i \qquad\qquad i = i\ (1, \ldots, n) \qquad (1.5)$$

where X_k equals the value of the kth aggregate factor, the value of X_k is irrelevant so long as that country imports commodities that require heavy inputs of the domestically scarce factor, and exports commodities intensively utilizing the domestically abundant factor. This crucial fact, which is not always well understood, means that the rationality of changes in the structure of domestic factor proportions associated with the introduction of foreign trade into a closed economy, under conditions to be elaborated shortly, depends only on relative domestic factor availabilities.

The demonstration of the statements above will be made with the aid of the Edgeworth-Bowley box in Figure 1-1. Two factors are depicted, capital and labor, which are used in industries A and B with corresponding origins 0 and 0'. Any point within the box represents a potential distribution of factors between A and B. The locus of efficient factor combinations is shown by the curvilinear contract curve through both origins. Such a contract curve, in contradistinction to the linear locus also drawn in Figure 1-1, implies that factors are not combined in fixed proportions in both industries. Moreover, since the curvilinear contract curve never crosses the diagonal, factor intensity reversals are ruled out by assumption. One industry will always be relatively labor intensive, while the other is capital intensive. If we start at the before-trade equilibrium point Ω,

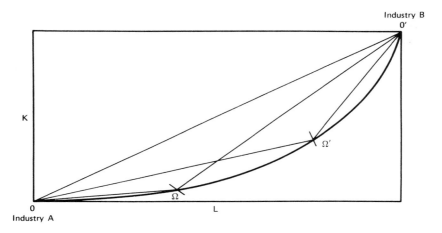

Figure 1-1. HECKSCHER-OHLIN THEOREM I. Adjustment of Domestic Factor Proportions With the Opening of Foreign Trade.

where the isoquants of both industries are tangent, we find that industry A is labor intensive and B capital intensive. If labor is the abundant factor, the opening up of trade according to the Heckscher-Ohlin approach, where comparative advantage is determined by domestic factor proportions, should result in the exportation of the abundant factor intensive commodity A, and the importation of B. The corresponding increase in A's output and contraction in B's is shown by the shift of resource allocation between the two industries from Ω to Ω'. At Ω' we see by inspection of the slopes of the various rays from the two origins that the capital intensity of both industries has increased, with the result that the factor price ratio has shifted in favor of labor. This is the familiar Heckscher-Ohlin result for a single country. The change in factor price relatives is purely an internal technological matter, no labor actually leaves the country. With the increased production of the labor intensive good A, factors must be obtained from B, assuming full employment. But B is the capital intensive industry. For every unit contraction of output in B, more capital will be released than labor. The price of labor will rise while the price of capital will fall, resulting in increased capital intensity in both industries. This means, as initially stated, the efficiency of factor utilization, given international factor immobility, will depend on adjustments in the domestic factor structure attendant on the opening of foreign trade. From what has just been said it should be clear that as long as internal commodity prices are determined by underlying factor availabilities the domestic adjustment for international factor immobility will always manifest itself by the increased utilization intensity of the scarce factor and an increased return to the abundant factor. If we were to observe the opposite result in any given country, this outcome would suggest either the falsification of the Heckscher-Ohlin conjecture that underlying factor availabilities are the ultimate determinates of comparative advantage, or that domestic factor adjustment processes were irrational.

Our discussion of the Heckscher-Ohlin approach to factor analysis given international factor immobility has revealed that the rationality of factor adjustment after the opening of trade will depend on the direction of change in domestic factor proportions. The beauty of this approach is that it avoids the awkward problems encumbent in the net embodied factor flow alternative. We can assess the rationality of the factor adjustment process without ever having to make implausible assumptions about the factor content value of imported goods. So important is the place of the factor proportions notion in the Heckscher-Ohlin approach that I would suggest that the Heckscher-Ohlin theorem be decomposed into two parts. Theorem I would assert that comparative advantage is ultimately determined by factor availabilities, and that trade therefore will result in domestic factor proportion changes of the sort described above. Theorem II would contain the general factor price equalization theorem which asserts not only that Theorem I holds without exception in all countries of the world, but that under a set of rigid conditions factor prices will be equalized globally in all countries as well. Before discussing Theorem II in greater detail, it should be emphasized that these theorems are separable. Regardless of the plausibility of Theorem II, Theorem I, stressing as it does rational factor utilization, is applicable for any economic system, and thereby constitutes a major justification for undertaking a factor proportions analysis of the U.S.S.R.

D. Factor Price Equalization

Although the Heckscher-Ohlin theorem is in reality two theorems, in the recent literature on factor analysis Theorem I has been subsumed under the more theoretically tenuous notion of factor price equalization found in Theorem II. Thus, the factor price equalization process is usually presented in the form illustrated in Figure 1-2, in a two country, two commodity, two factor world model. Each country is represented by an Edgeworth-Bowley Box with a commodity origin for industry A at 0. Industry B's origin is located at $0'$ in country I and $0''$ for country II. The before-trade production points are η and Ω. Factors at these points are combined in extremely different proportions so that the corresponding factor price ratios are accordingly diverse. Since according to Theorem I commodity prices are determined by the prevailing factor availabilities, country I will have a comparative advantage in the production of

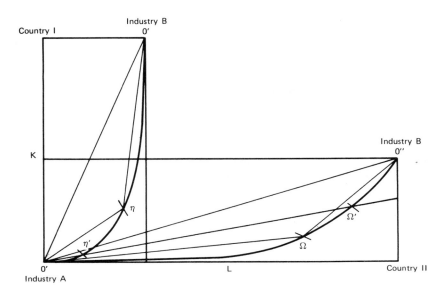

Figure 1-2. FACTOR PRICE EQUALIZATION: The Two Country Case.

industry B and country II in the production of A. The full factor price equalization theorem implies that with the opening of trade country I will expand its production of B from η', while country II increases its output of A from Ω to Ω'. A ray from the industry A origin has been drawn to pass through η' and Ω' indicating that the capital labor ratio for industry A is identical in both countries and that factor prices have been equalized internationally, so that there exists no opportunity cost advantage to further changes in the structure of commodity flows.

Gottfried Haberler gives seven conditions which are required for this result to obtain.

1. free competition in all markets
2. absence of transportation costs
3. all commodities continue to be produced in both countries after free trade has begun
4. production functions in both countries are identical and homogeneous in the first degree
5. the production function must be such that one commodity is always labor intensive and the other always capital intensive, that is there are no factor intensity reversals
6. factors of production are qualitatively the same in all countries
7. the number of factors is not greater than the number of commodities.[3]

This is a formidable list of requirements which are not likely to be realized in the real world. Noting the implausibility of these conditions, Haberler concludes that the factor price equalization hypothesis can hardly be regarded as a valuable contribution to economic theory. But he is careful to discern that the factor price equalization hypothesis is only a part of the Heckscher-Ohlin analysis. He points out that the rejection of Heckscher-Ohlin Theorem II does not impugn the reasonableness of Theorem I.

Ohlin's more modest and somewhat unprecise contention, of which he himself admitted the possibility of exceptions, to the effect that trade will tend to bring about a partial equilization of factor prices would, however, seem to be valid as any empirical proposition.[4]

Thus, Theorem I may be empirically valid for many or even most countries, because it does not depend on the extremely implausible assumptions predicated for the factor price equalization case.

This brief discussion of the factor price equalization extension of the Heckscher-Ohlin hypothesis has been undertaken only to emphasize that our study of Soviet factor proportions neither stands nor falls on Haberler's implausible seven conditions. Our analysis refers to the Heckscher-Ohlin theorem only in the first sense distinguished.

E. The Leontief Statistic

The fundamental empirical measure used in this study to measure factor proportions is the Leontief Statistic.[5] It is a ratio of the two factor ratios shown in Equation (1.6).

$$\Omega = \frac{K^m/L^m}{K^e/L^e} \qquad (1.6)$$

where Ω = Leontief Statistic.

The numerator refers to the direct-plus-indirect aggregate factors required to produce one million dollars' worth of import-competing replacements. Computing each term separately in Equations (1.7) and (1.8), k_i represents the coefficient of direct and indirect capital required to sustain the output of each import replacement commodity q_i^m, and l_i the direct-plus-indirect labor requirements similarly defined.

$$K^m = \sum_{i=1}^{n} k_i q_i^m \qquad (1.7)$$

where K^m = capital embodied in import replacements,

$$L^m = \sum_{i=1}^{n} l_i q_i^m \qquad (1.8)$$

and L^m = labor embodied in import replacements. The specification of import replacements as opposed to imports is not accidental. It is usually thought that data limitations necessitated the use of import replacements because in the multi-country case the embodied factors in a given import bundle would be a weighted average of all the factors embodied in each nation's share of all the various commodities imported. This indeed is a formidable requirement, but as we saw in Figure 1-1 the empirical difficulty entailed in computing the embodied factor content of commodities originating in a host of different countries is a superfluous consideration because according to Heckscher-Ohlin I it is domestic factor proportions and not net factor flows that count. Thus, a great, and too often unrecognized, merit of the Leontief Statistic is that it handles factor proportions in the import sector in precisely the correct theoretical manner implied by the Heckscher-Ohlin theorem.

The denominator of the Leontief Statistic represents the factors embodied directly and indirectly in a million dollars' worth of exports. The capital and labor requirements of the export industry are computed according to formulas

(1.9 and 1.10) where k_i and l_i have the same meaning as in Equations (1.7 and 1.8), and q_i^e refers to the ith export good.

$$K^e = \sum_{i=1}^{n} k_i q_i^e \tag{1.9}$$

where K^e = capital embodied in exports,

$$L^e = \sum_{i=1}^{n} l_i q_i^e \tag{1.10}$$

and L^e = labor embodied in exports.

In the theoretical literature great importance is placed on whether the Leontief Statistic is greater than, equal to, or less than 1.

$$\Omega = \frac{K^m/L^m}{K^e/L^e} \begin{array}{c} > \\ < \end{array} 1 \tag{1.11}$$

The emphasis given to this inequality, or equality, as the case may be is well founded because it tells us the exact effect of trade on factor proportions. $\Omega > 1$ means that import replacements are more capital intensive than exports; $\Omega = 1$ that import replacements and exports are produced with the same capital labor ratios; and $\Omega < 1$ that import replacements are less capital intensive than exports. However, it is not always clearly understood that a given Leontief Statistic is compatible with a variety of factor combinations. Take the case where $\Omega > 1$. This result can be obtained under any of the following circumstances:

$$K^m > K^e \text{ and } L^m < L^e \tag{1.12}$$

$$K^m > K^e, L^m > L^e \tag{1.13}$$

$$\text{and } K^m/K^e > L^m/L^e$$

$$K^m < K^e, L^m < L^e \tag{1.14}$$

$$\text{and } K^m/K^e > L^m/L^e$$

The conditions expressed in Equation (1.12) correspond with the usual interpretation of Heckscher-Ohlin. As a result of international trade the abundant factor intensive good is exported, and the scarce factor intensive good imported. On balance capital is imported in embodied form and labor exported.

But this need not be so. Condition (1.13) shows that both capital and labor may be embodied more intensively in import replacements, while condition (1.14) illustrates the case where both factors are more intensively embodied in exports. Thus, both factors may simultaneously be embodied more or less intensively in import replacements than exports, with a Leontief Statistic greater than one, implying that the embodied factor intensity of each factor is not specific to either import replacements or exports. This result is perfectly consistent with the factor proportions approach where relative and not absolute scarcities are theoretically crucial. It is even consistent with the net embodied factor flow approach. Our interest in distinguishing these cases is to bring out the complex nature of the Leontief statistic often glossed over in causal exposition where the impression is frequently given that the import replacements are associated with an absolutely greater embodiment of one factor and exports an absolutely greater embodiment of the other.

Two additional points can be briefly made. First, the choice of a million rubles of import replacements and exports as representative traded bundles of goods is intended to represent a marginal change in the aggregate mix of goods and services produced by the economy. The larger the change in the structure of trade, the more dubious becomes the assumption of constant technological coefficients underlying input-output analysis. Second, the Leontief Statistic by itself cannot tell us anything about the rationality of the factor proportions adjustment process triggered by a change in the structure of foreign trade. To ascertain whether a given factor proportions adjustment is Heckscher-Ohlin I rational, we must be able to determine whether the country in question vis-à-vis its trading partners and the world as a whole is capital or labor rich.

2

The 1959 Soviet Input-Output Table and Other Data Sources

In a study of the sort undertaken here questions of data sources, data quality, and data adjustment are of the first significance. The basic data input into our analysis was determined by the techniques chosen for the computation of the statistics ultimately desired. For the factor proportions analysis the Soviet input-output table is the primary data source, while official Soviet trade statistics are the key element in the study of commodity flows. Since the official foreign trade statistics play an important role in factor proportions analysis as well as commodity flows, we will treat both major data sources together under the input-output heading.

A. The Soviet 1959 Input-Output Table

Input-output analysis is a relatively new discipline. Although enormous strides have been made in the field, fundamental data problems continue to be of concern, even in the United States. Therefore, the utilization of the input-output approach to deal with theoretical issues touching on the Soviet economy must be undertaken cautiously. Pioneering work on the construction of an input-output table began in the United States in the 1930s under the direction of Wassily Leontief. By contrast practical work with input-output techniques did not begin in the Soviet Union until the mid-1950s, when experiments were simultaneously and secretly conducted by the Economic Research Institute of Gosplan and the Laboratory of Mathematical Methods in Economic Research and Planning of the Academy of Sciences of the U.S.S.R. under the direction of V.S. Nemchinov.[1] From these rudimentary beginnings, the Soviets were able to produce an 83 sector square I-O table in 1960. A 38 sector version of this table for 1959 appears in Table 2-1.

B. The Intersectoral Flow Matrix

The input-output table was divided into four quadrants. The first quadrant describing intersectoral flows was constructed with data obtained from a stratified random-sampling survey, covering 20 percent of all industrial and construction enterprises, undertaken between April and June, 1960.[2] Data for nonindustrial sectors was obtained from traditional Central Statistical Adminis-

15

Table 2-1
Reconstructed 1959 Soviet Input-Output Table
a. Interindustry Transactions Matrix
(Product in Millions of Current Rubles; Employment in Thousands of Man Years)

Using Sector Producing Sector	Ferrous Ores	Ferrous Metals	Nonferrous Ores	Nonferrous Metals	Coking Coal	Metal Products
	1	2	3	4	5	6
1 Ferrous ores	0.9	291.5	0.	47.3	0.	28.0
2 Ferrous metals	8.6	854.2	15.9	0.	1.6	406.5
3 Nonferrous ores	0.	0.	0.8	798.4	0.	0.
4 Nonferrous metals	0.	552.7	0.	551.5	0.	5.8
5 Coking coal	6.0	735.0	0.	154.1	91.3	16.7
6 Metal products	3.8	89.8	3.2	22.8	0.8	31.3
7	13.9	525.6	10.8	34.1	968.6	18.0
8 Oil	3.1	101.6	22.6	71.7	1.6	14.2
9 Gas	0.1	2.4	0.5	1.7	0.9	1.4
10 Other fuels	0.	0.2	0.1	0.1	18.2	0.1
11 Electrical power	25.1	92.9	12.3	201.5	35.2	30.5
12 Electrical & power M&E	1.5	7.0	2.1	2.3	0.6	0.7
13 Tools & instruments	3.3	15.5	4.7	5.1	0.5	7.7
14 General machinery	9.4	43.9	13.3	14.6	0.5	4.3
15 Transportation M&E	0.3	1.6	0.5	0.5	0.	0.2
16 Automobiles	0.8	3.8	1.1	1.3	0.	1.0
17 Agricultural M&E	0.3	1.3	0.4	0.5	0.	0.1
18 Machinery n.e.c.	0.	0.	0.	0.	0.	0.
19 Metal working	1.3	5.8	1.6	1.9	0.2	1.5
20 Repair of machinery	21.9	101.7	30.8	33.9	3.3	4.9
21 Abrasives	1.2	3.2	1.7	1.1	0.	1.3
22 Mineral & basic chemls	6.4	39.0	9.1	13.0	15.5	3.3
23 Synthetics, paints	2.5	14.7	3.4	4.9	0.5	2.3
24 Rubber products	2.5	15.3	3.5	5.1	0.7	1.7
25 Lumber & woodworking	14.3	38.6	20.0	12.9	0.9	15.3
26 Paper	0.6	1.6	0.9	0.5	0.1	9.8
27 Construction materials	2.3	6.3	3.3	2.1	0.2	1.6
28 Glass	0.5	1.2	0.6	0.4	0.1	0.2
29 Textiles	1.4	8.7	1.9	2.9	0.3	22.8
30 Apparel and footwear	8.0	51.5	11.3	17.2	3.6	15.9
31 Food	1.0	6.2	1.3	2.1	0.6	0.4
32 Industry n.e.c.	0.	0.	0.	0.	0.	0.
33 Construction	0.	0.	0.	0.	0.	0.
34 Agriculture	0.	0.6	0.	0.8	0.	0.3
35 Forestry	0.	0.	0.	0.	0.	0.
36 Transport. and comm.	80.0	400.0	35.2	140.9	44.3	57.3
37 Trade & distribution	19.0	219.4	27.3	129.6	0.	30.7
38 Products n.e.c.	0.	88.7	0.	88.6	0.	0.
39 Total purchases	240.0	4321.5	240.4	2365.4	1190.1	735.8
40 Depreciation	57.8	296.0	73.0	167.6	45.8	32.4
41 Labor income	188.3	1073.6	238.4	754.2	103.1	200.8
42 Other net income	76.0	522.1	−44.9	378.3	12.7	7.2
43 National income	264.3	1595.7	193.5	1132.5	115.8	208.0
44 Imports	0.	256.8	320.6	164.5	0.	0.
45 Total outlays	562.1	6470.0	627.5	3830.0	1351.7	976.2
46 Employment	147.7	697.9	130.7	328.9	43.9	100.5
47 Capital	1,322	5,369	2,194	1,991	725	747

Coal	Oil	Gas	Other Fuels	Electrical Power	Electrical & pwr M&E	Tools & instruments	General Machinery
7	8	9	10	11	12	13	14
0.	0.	0.	0.	0.	0.	0.	0.
28.8	9.9	0.6	3.0	3.5	374.0	176.6	650.6
0.	0.	0.	0.	0.	0.	0.	0.
2.8	1.2	0.	0.5	0.9	183.2	484.6	145.8
0.3	6.8	0.1	0.	0.	3.0	0.8	21.5
13.2	2.5	0.1	1.6	2.2	19.7	31.7	58.5
841.2	0.1	10.5	6.8	796.	19.0	7.8	28.6
7.9	1066.5	4.1	11.7	245.5	24.3	11.9	46.5
0.1	1.4	0.1	0.3	68.	0.4	0.5	0.7
0.1	0.2	10.6	20.8	231.7	1.0	0.3	15.0
138.8	173.8	2.0	22.3	4.	45.5	31.3	76.1
6.1	1.1	0.2	2.0	8.	191.2	29.6	210.3
27.2	3.2	0.3	4.7	3.	127.1	129.5	111.0
57.1	22.3	0.4	7.8	0.	2.3	1.9	198.6
0.6	0.	0.	1.5	0.	0.	0.4	12.5
0.5	1.1	0.1	0.7	0.	3.1	8.2	126.2
0.7	1.7	0.	4.6	0.	18.5	0.	87.8
88.3	28.0	1.0	20.4	21.0	25.3	6.6	91.5
10.1	0.7	0.	0.5	1.1	20.7	2.9	33.8
2.1	32.3	2.0	1.3	59.0	6.5	7.0	12.6
0.3	0.1	0.	0.1	0.1	47.3	8.4	5.3
4.2	41.2	0.4	2.3	3.5	15.5	6.1	10.3
1.7	16.1	1.2	0.7	1.4	72.4	95.0	41.1
26.9	1.2	0.1	3.0	0.8	21.4	15.3	85.8
396.5	5.1	0.5	13.6	2.9	28.2	32.9	59.1
0.5	0.8	0.	0.1	0.2	11.5	9.6	3.7
11.9	4.4	0.2	0.8	1.8	5.6	2.4	7.5
0.5	0.3	0.	0.1	0.4	13.5	12.6	1.8
1.9	1.0	0.1	0.6	1.0	30.5	34.2	9.8
132.3	9.0	0.8	15.3	9.5	13.8	19.4	39.8
1.7	1.9	0.1	0.3	1.5	4.7	3.2	3.8
0.4	0.	0.	0.	0.	22.8	20.7	38.0
0.	0.	0.	0.	0.	0.	0.	0.
2.6	0.1	0.	0.2	0.	0.2	0.1	0.3
0.	0.	0.	0.	0.	0.	0.	0.
1528.2	1184.1	0.2	66.5	4.8	58.7	44.0	195.2
146.2	680.8	14.4	1.5	8.3	36.7	63.5	18.8
0.	0.	0.	0.	0.	4.8	3.9	17.1
3481.3	3298.9	50.1	215.6	1484.0	1452.4	1302.9	2465.0
307.2	300.0	17.4	44.5	500.1	95.0	83.7	157.6
3035.6	287.7	16.3	260.9	426.6	759.9	669.4	1260.6
−526.2	2675.4	182.5	29.0	1163.3	99.7	1863.4	−115.5
2509.4	2963.1	198.5	289.9	1591.9	859.6	2532.8	1145.1
83.1	141.0	0.	0.	0.	95.1	133.6	596.9
6381.0	6703.0	266.0	550.0	3576.0	3502.1	4053.0	4364.6
1253.6	176.5	14.2	245.3	405.4	473.0	588.3	860.1
7548	4926	589	693	10,611	1217	957	2,676

Table 2-1 (cont.)

Using Sector	Transportation M&E	Automatics	Agricultural M&E	Machinery N.E.C.	Metal Working	Repair of Machinery	Abrasives
Producing Sector	15	16	17	18	19	20	21
1 Ferrous ores	0.	0.	0.	0.	0.	0.	2.0
2 Ferrous metals	192.8	220.4	292.6	50.0	564.4	343.3	1.7
3 Nonferrous ores	0.	0.	0.	0.	0.	0.	2.5
4 Nonferrous metals	48.1	146.6	31.6	50.0	83.7	118.7	2.5
5 Coking coal	2.5	6.6	9.3	1.9	30.5	12.6	1.2
6 Metal products	14.2	37.3	26.0	13.9	39.4	50.4	0.5
7	17.8	14.9	9.0	9.1	14.2	50.3	3.1
8 Oil	16.0	25.4	14.6	13.0	10.9	59.7	4.4
9 Gas	0.5	0.6	0.7	0.3	0.4	0.9	0.1
10 Other fuels	2.8	0.5	0.4	1.9	2.8	1.4	0.
11 Electrical power	22.4	20.1	40.6	34.3	26.3	59.2	8.9
12 Electrical & power M&E	228.4	18.0	19.5	278.8	16.3	58.0	0.2
13 Tools & instruments	33.6	37.5	49.8	197.8	12.7	88.2	0.6
14 General machinery	11.9	1.1	3.6	11.6	2.0	20.7	0.1
15 Transportation M&E	91.2	0.	0.	7.1	0.	65.2	0.
16 Automobiles	8.6	315.1	11.4	86.7	3.7	252.0	0.
17 Agricultural M&E	3.6	0.1	217.5	60.4	2.2	204.2	0.
18 Machinery n.e.c.	47.7	9.5	14.0	136.3	0.	50.0	0.
19 Metal working	42.1	14.7	3.7	0.	46.6	43.7	0.4
20 Repair of machinery	6.1	6.4	2.4	0.	3.1	0.	2.8
21 Abrasives	3.9	3.2	3.4	0.	2.2	3.1	8.6
22 Mineral & basic chemls	5.0	6.4	3.1	7.9	6.4	10.1	3.7
23 Synthetics, paints	25.8	36.2	17.9	48.6	35.2	64.4	0.3
24 Rubber products	16.4	375.8	92.2	38.9	5.0	23.8	0.2
25 Lumber & woodworking	56.7	26.9	33.7	35.4	15.0	107.3	0.5
26 Paper	1.0	3.7	1.6	4.6	2.0	3.9	0.4
27 Construction materials	14.7	2.6	2.0	0.	5.0	30.0	0.5
28 Glass	3.5	13.8	0.7	0.	4.6	6.3	0.1
29 Textiles	16.0	18.0	14.1	35.0	6.4	27.6	11.8
30 Apparel and footwear	16.5	35.2	18.1	0.	20.0	27.4	1.1
31 Food	2.2	2.1	1.1	0.	1.8	3.3	2.7
32 Industry n.e.c.	15.1	25.3	18.1	17.6	0.	0.	0.
33 Construction	0.	0.	0.	0.	0.	0.	0.
34 Agriculture	0.5	0.	0.	0.	0.1	0.2	0.
35 Forestry	0.	0.	0.	0.	0.	0.	0.
36 Transport. and comm.	17.6	116.6	131.8	23.0	238.1	17.0	4.5
37 Trade & distribution	0.	51.7	49.2	77.1	102.9	0.	0.
38 Products n.e.c.	8.5	2.8	16.2	8.0	18.6	7.4	0.
39 Total purchases	994.6	1595.1	1149.9	1249.2	1322.5	1810.3	65.5
40 Depreciation	68.4	57.1	67.8	166.7	68.7	125.5	3.1
41 Labor income	547.1	442.3	426.3	1436.8	549.6	1004.2	32.1
42 Other net income	−75.6	939.6	775.5	2234.9	948.9	810.0	22.3
43 National income	471.5	1381.9	1201.8	3671.7	1498.5	1814.2	54.4
44 Imports	475.5	49.9	10.5	23.7	5.3	0.	1.6
45 Total outlays	2010.0	3084.0	2430.0	5111.3	2895.0	3750.0	124.6
46 Employment	535.0	347.0	423.0	1240.8	677.3	1236.0	27.7
47 Capital	1,423	1,161	1,053	2,101	664	2,434	94

Mineral & Basic Chemls	Synthetics, Paints	Rubber Products	Lumber & Woodworking	Paper	Construction Materials	Glass	Textiles	Apparel & Footwear	Food
22	23	24	25	26	27	28	29	30	31
1.7	0.	0.	0.	0.	4.7	6.2	0.	0.	0.
7.0	18.0	3.7	18.1	5.4	199.6	5.0	7.8	2.7	69.1
3.0	0.	0.	0.	0.	22.8	0.	0.	0.	0.
10.0	124.7	3.9	3.0	1.9	47.3	4.0	2.5	2.7	18.4
43.2	49.1	0.2	45.2	0.1	13.2	0.1	0.5	0.1	0.5
5.5	3.2	7.4	55.4	1.9	42.8	10.7	9.5	12.9	12.4
25.6	46.4	4.8	18.7	47.1	251.1	24.5	53.0	17.1	182.5
15.1	124.2	14.4	231.1	13.0	148.5	20.4	20.4	12.4	194.7
0.6	16.9	0.2	0.4	0.1	12.7	0.9	1.2	0.3	4.4
0.4	1.6	0.2	27.5	9.6	27.8	13.9	21.3	8.0	15.1
66.7	100.3	26.8	17.8	42.7	223.8	13.4	112.5	48.6	111.5
1.9	3.9	0.5	6.8	1.0	4.9	0.9	3.9	2.4	5.6
3.5	3.7	2.8	21.7	2.4	23.5	1.6	5.9	3.3	10.3
7.0	6.0	1.7	21.2	6.3	36.4	1.1	40.8	9.6	24.0
0.1	0.1	0.	2.6	0.	0.1	0.	0.	0.	0.4
1.9	0.7	1.6	7.7	0.5	20.9	0.4	1.5	0.6	4.1
0.3	0.1	0.	7.4	0.1	7.2	0.1	0.4	0.	0.6
10.8	10.6	4.8	0.	0.	92.7	0.	0.	0.	82.0
3.1	11.7	3.9	2.1	3.0	15.6	11.2	20.8	28.3	57.3
10.6	33.3	3.2	7.1	3.4	89.5	24.5	14.4	5.5	229.2
0.1	1.1	0.1	5.1	0.1	1.0	1.5	0.2	1.5	0.2
151.6	206.1	4.4	15.0	18.4	4.7	2.1	0.2	11.3	27.7
36.5	975.2	619.0	79.6	3.4	10.9	11.1	334.7	208.0	43.3
2.2	12.9	209.7	41.4	1.3	20.5	0.9	28.9	28.0	7.3
14.9	80.8	17.1	240.3	324.6	122.2	31.4	45.5	74.0	289.3
7.8	45.7	1.1	5.3	80.1	26.2	4.3	6.9	17.3	73.8
3.5	3.6	0.9	11.3	6.8	1273.4	7.0	6.8	3.7	25.3
1.2	27.5	0.2	.6	0.4	0.9	13.0	0.7	0.9	49.4
7.8	57.9	395.1	243.1	8.4	9.8	5.8	6206.7	6981.9	85.6
20.2	22.5	5.1	154.1	6.1	42.6	9.1	25.2	2154.3	108.8
20.2	405.6	7.0	31.0	1.3	7.8	0.8	20.5	599.6	13365.8
5.3	13.4	7.5	0.	0.	92.8	0.	25.0	25.0	0.
0.	0.	0.	0.	0.	0.	0.	0.	0.	0.
0.3	11.5	0.	32.6	1.1	0.6	0.3	3980.3	490.5	16467.3
0.	0.	0.	142.8	0.	0.	0.	0.	0.	0.
514.0	35.1	55.8	1626.1	72.9	1726.1	86.0	284.7	159.6	1212.3
21.7	49.1	17.3	404.4	89.5	338.7	88.5	700.3	703.7	3681.6
0.	55.3	10.7	0.	78.1	51.5	10.7	0.	97.9	80.7
1025.3	2557.8	1431.1	6343.5	831.0	5014.8	411.4	11983.0	11711.7	36540.5
44.1	148.4	13.6	363.0	40.1	316.6	21.3	110.0	110.0	443.1
195.8	593.7	176.5	3020.5	200.6	1794.3	232.2	923.8	1410.3	2531.7
65.8	1151.6	361.3	1236.4	181.2	141.2	204.5	11454.1	1987.7	16893.7
261.6	1745.3	537.8	4256.9	381.8	1935.5	436.7	12377.9	3398.0	19425.4
26.0	261.5	17.5	198.6	14.1	37.1	8.0	1229.1	2280.3	1390.6
1357.0	4713.0	2000.0	11031.0	1267.0	7304.0	877.4	25700.0	17500.0	57800.0
132.1	431.1	100.0	2852.8	147.0	1623.3	214.3	1820.0	1920.0	2530.0
1,062	2,393	292	3,858	878	4,537	399	2,880	1,129	8,016

Table 2-1 (cont.)

Using Sector	Industry N.E.C.	Construction	Agriculture	Forestry	Transport. & comm.	Trade & distribution
Producing Sector	32	33	34	35	36	37
1 Ferrous ores	0.	0.	0.	0.	0.	0.
2 Ferrous metals	70.0	1365.0	5.5	0.	63.7	57.5
3 Nonferrous ores	0.	0.	0.	0.	0.	0.
4 Nonferrous metals	30.0	21.7	0.3	0.	23.1	16.2
5 Coking coal	0.	0.	0.	0.	0.2	0.
6 Metal products	0.	232.6	12.1	0.2	38.0	21.0
7	20.8	49.5	11.7	0.	803.0	68.6
8 Oil	20.9	366.5	1051.7	5.1	961.6	32.6
9 Gas	0.5	9.7	0.	0.	0.	0.
10 Other fuels	1.9	8.5	0.3	0.	0.	0.
11 Electrical power	60.7	200.6	88.3	0.	150.2	42.1
12 Electrical & power M&E	34.4	127.3	38.8	0.	4.1	14.8
13 Tools & instruments	45.5	551.1	11.8	0.	29.	9.6
14 General machinery	23.7	84.0	0.	0.	2.	49.1
15 Transportation M&E	11.5	6.4	3.5	0.	152.	0.
16 Automobiles	38.4	70.6	19.0	0.	20.8	0.
17 Agricultural M&E	27.7	45.4	159.0	3.5	5.	0.
18 Machinery n.e.c.	61.0	228.8	414.9	0.	6.0	136.7
19 Metal working	62.8	1208.9	156.6	3.1	.	3.7
20 Repair of machinery	64.7	0.	1028.1	0.	1.3	0.
21 Abrasives	0.	9.5	5.2	0.	0.	1.5
22 Mineral & basic chemls	80.3	17.7	355.6	2.7	9.2	7.5
23 Synthetics, paints	237.7	203.8	55.4	0.	31.7	12.0
24 Rubber products	121.4	69.3	12.6	0.	59.9	54.4
25 Lumber & woodworking	64.6	2982.3	113.5	1.1	171.1	205.0
26 Paper	95.4	32.6	0.1	0.4	3.1	582.0
27 Construction materials	0.	5360.9	16.2	0.9	60.5	0.2
28 Glass	0.	319.3	5.1	0.	5.9	0.
29 Textiles	9.4	29.9	46.2	0.	74.1	398.6
30 Apparel and footwear	0.	535.5	99.8	0.2	70.8	39.1
31 Food	319.7	85.2	1582.4	0.	0.	11.3
32 Industry n.e.c.	0.	0.	128.3	0.	0.	0.
33 Construction	0.	0.	0.	0.	0.	0.
34 Agriculture	207.8	11.2	12436.5	4.1	19.0	0.
35 Forestry	0.	66.5	0.	6.	0.	0.
36 Transport. and comm.	43.8	38.9	762.2	5.0	49.2	116.5
37 Trade & distribution	722.7	0.	2857.6	0.	0.	0.
38 Products n.e.c.	292.0	270.7	6.0	0.	0.	0.
39 Total purchases	3271.3	14009.9	21484.3	32.9	3466.2	1930.0
40 Depreciation	125.2	579.0	2100.0	0.	1195.0	434.0
41 Labor income	701.3	7021.9	23800.0	275.1	4853.0	3827.6
42 Other net income	1383.5	6989.2	4815.7	0.	1742.0	5172.3
43 National income	2084.8	14011.1	28615.7	275.	6595.0	8999.9
44 Imports	49.1	0.	1300.0	0.	0.	0.
45 Total outlays	5530.4	29200.0	53500.0	308.	11256.2	11363.9
46 Employment	600.0	6208.0	33100.0	352.	5300.0	5171.0
47 Capital	4,900	5,455	42,925	15	28,942	7,512

Products N.E.C.	Total Interindustry Use	Private Consumption	Public Consumption	Gross Investment	Exports	Total Final Demand	Total Gross Output
38	39	40	41	42	43	44	45
0.	382.3	0.	0.	−21.1	200.9	179.8	562.1
1.8	6099.0	2.1	20.0	−183.4	532.3	371.0	6470.0
0.	827.5	0.	0.	−15.2	15.2	0.	827.5
0.2	2720.1	2.1	292.3	619.8	195.7	1109.9	3830.0
0.	1253.0	0.	0.	68.3	30.4	98.7	1351.7
2.5	931.0	12.8	40.4	−18.0	10.0	45.2	976.2
2.9	5037.6	146.3	542.2	426.1	228.8	1343.4	6381.0
3.5	5063.3	103.2	360.7	609.4	566.4	1639.7	6703.0
0.	130.3	49.8	36.0	48.2	1.7	135.7	266.0
0.	444.3	0.	60.2	45.5	0.	105.7	550.0
2.6	2442.1	635.5	397.3	101.1	0.	1133.9	3576.0
1.1	1334.7	329.3	57.0	727.6	53.5	1167.4	2502.1
0.1	1589.0	605.1	56.9	1377.9	424.1	2464.0	4053.0
0.	741.1	234.0	0.2	3012.8	376.5	3623.5	4364.6
0.	358.5	0.	35.8	1525.5	90.2	1651.5	2010.0
0.7	1261.4	555.7	74.9	1030.3	161.7	1822.6	3084.0
0.	907.3	0.	0.	1421.3	101.4	1522.7	2430.0
0.	1650.9	578.3	166.5	2700.9	14.7	3460.4	5111.3
0.	1915.6	859.1	188.4	−68.1	0.	979.4	2895.0
0.	1980.5	0.	19.8	1749.7	0.	1769.5	3750.0
0.	121.6	0.	0.	2.5	0.5	3.0	124.6
0.1	1128.3	42.4	43.4	31.5	111.4	228.7	1357.0
11.8	3382.4	357.1	402.1	518.5	52.9	1330.6	4713.0
2.9	1729.2	34.5	132.0	92.7	11.6	270.8	2000.0
2.0	8166.0	1271.6	424.9	920.9	249.6	2867.0	11033.0
163.5	1202.7	0.	81.2	−33.2	16.3	64.3	1267.0
0.1	6886.3	122.9	274.6	9.8	10.4	417.7	7304.0
0.	525.3	333.7	17.6	−2.1	2.9	352.1	877.4
23.2	14789.5	9287.0	337.2	1115.4	170.9	10910.5	25700.0
1.1	3810.2	10205.9	439.0	2988.1	56.8	13689.8	17500.0
0.	17000.2	35575.0	1214.4	3138.1	872.3	40799.8	57800.0
0.	454.9	4805.1	610.7	−381.3	41.0	5075.5	5530.4
0.	0.	0.	0.	29200.0	0.	29200.0	29200.0
0.	33669.5	17096.9	515.7	1557.9	660.0	19830.5	53500.0
15.8	231.3	0.	0.	76.7	0.	76.7	308.0
80.0	11256.2	0.	0.	0.	0.	0.0	11256.2
11.7	11363.9	0.	0.	0.	0.	0.0	11363.9
0.	1218.2	1929.6	157.9	−309.9	4.2	1781.	3000.0
327.6	154005.2	85175.0	6999.3	54084.2	5264.3	151522.8	105524.0
266.0	8983.8	2825.5	2094.5	0.	0.	4920.0	
1563.7	66835.8						
842.7	66603.2						
2406.4	133439.0						
0.	9100.0						
3000.0	305528.0						
1709.0	73983.4						
411	166,104						

Sources: Vladimir Treml, "The 1959 Soviet Input-Output Table in NEW DIRECTIONS IN THE SOVIET ECONOMY, JEC, 1966, 268a, and Vladimir Treml, "New Soviet Inter-industry Data," in SOVIET ECONOMIC PERFORMANCE 1966-67, JEC, 1968, 147.

tration sources. For certain nonindustrial sectors, reliance on traditional data sources is of little consequence because of the general homogeneity of their output, which makes special detailed sampling superfluous. Thus Treml argues that the failure to extend the survey to such nonindustrial sectors as transportation, communications, distribution, forestry, and other branches is of little consequence. This, however, is not true for agriculture, and the notorious deficiencies in the cost calculations of Sovkhozy and Kolkhozy must surely be the sources of some substantial, but unmeasurable degree of error.[3] Besides the error introduced by the use of traditional data of questionable applicability, in evaluating the accuracy of the Soviet input-output table we are also confronted with the issue of the inherent statistical reliability of the stratified-random industrial survey. Quoting various Soviet sources Treml identifies three areas of potential difficulty regarding the sampling survey. First, it is not known whether the 20 percent target sample was actually achieved. Second, only one criterion of representativeness was used to define which enterprises would be included in any specific stratum: the value of the mean gross output of each subclass had to coincide with the mean gross output of the entire class. The defect in this statistical procedure reposes in the fact that there is no obvious correspondence between the input structure of subclasses with the same mean gross value of output. Third, sampled enterprises tended to fill out the relevant questionnaires with estimates rather than actual cost data.[4] The seriousness of these defects cannot be calibrated. They do not by any means appear to render the construction of the 1959 Soviet I-O table futile, or meaningless, but they do underline the already suggested need for caution in evaluating empirical studies based on I-O techniques.

C. Classification

Accurate data, as essential as they may be, are only part of the problem of constructing a good input-output table. The classification scheme chosen is of almost equal importance. In evaluating the table as a whole and the intersectoral flow matrix in particular, it is important to recognize that the Soviets addressed the classification issue in an equivocal way. On one hand they elected to use the statistical classification employed by the Central Statistical Administration, which having evolved haphazardly over the years was ill-suited for the purposes of constructing homogenous product flows of the whole economy.[5] This choice was apparently dictated by the supplementary data requirements of the table builders. On the other hand, the Soviet input-output specialists went to great pains to construct pure product sectors, adopting techniques similar to those chosen by the Japanese in their intersectoral studies. Elaborate adjustment for all industrial sectors was made by separating out the value of output of secondary products, not primary to the given sector, and transferring these secondary outputs to their proper homogenous sector analogue. The primary input vectors were adjusted in the same manner. Since these adjustments required very detailed information, the sampling study was designed to obtain precisely this sort of information, not otherwise available. Treml considers the adjustments undertaken by the Soviet I-O specialists to be competently handled and impressive in their scope.[6] However, these pure sector adjustments, it should be fully understood, applied only to the industrial sectors. Outputs of the construction, agricultural and other nonindustrial sectors were left unaltered.

D. The Third Quadrant

Input-output tables, as mentioned before, can be divided conceptually into four quadrants. Intersectoral flows of intermediate goods appear in quadrant I, sometimes called the technology matrix. Final demand, normally classified into such macroeconomic aggregates as private consumption, government consumption, investment, and exports, fall under the quadrant II heading. Quadrant II houses the various elements of value added, imports, and primary factor inputs such as capital and labor, while quadrant IV accounts for the distribution of the various components of final demand among the value added categories. Our remarks on the data sources used in the construction of the Soviet input-output table have pertained thus far to quadrant I only. Quadrant II, however, poses no new problems. The data used in its construction were obtained from standard statistical sources without recourse to any special data accumulation effort. Exports require some further comment, but we will postpone the discussion in order to treat foreign trade in its entirety.

Quadrant III requires more extended consideration. The classification issue discussed in section C fortunately causes us no new difficulties, because the pure sector adjustments to intersectoral flows were extended consistently to the various components of value added.[7] The appropriate adjustments were made possible through the acquisition of detailed information on depreciation, turnover taxes, subsidies, labor income, and employment in the 20 percent stratified random industrial sampling. The quality and extent of publication of the data in quadrant III, however, varies greatly. Basically, quadrant III data come from standard statistical sources supplemented by the ancillary industrial sample. In one important instance, the capital stock, an additional source of information was utilized. I refer here to the 1959 economy-wide inventory and revaluation of capital. This capital survey was exceedingly thorough with the original capital stock table broken down in terms of 130 types of productive capital. Conceptually, however, no allowance was made for wear and tear and the figures represent initial cost adjusted for price changes.[8] It might be thought that, given the elaborate nature of the Soviet capital stock study, the depreciation data would be equally as good. Unfortunately, this is an incorrect surmise.

The depreciation data were prepared long before capital stock information was developed for input-output use, and is based on the 20 percent industrial sample. Moreover, the depreciation figures derived from the sample were accounting measures rather than actual depreciation cost statistics. An estimate of the global quality of the depreciation vector can be obtained from information supplied by Eidel'man to the effect that actual depreciation costs in 1959 for replacement as distinguished from repair were 47 percent greater than estimated by the traditional accounting methods. The discrepancy between nominal and actual depreciation for replacement and repair funds combined was 18 percent.[9] Given these serious discrepancies for the all-economy depreciation aggregates, Treml feels that the sectoral depreciation estimates in the input-output table are subject to enormous degrees of error and are therefore extremely unreliable.[10]

A further problem regarding the capital vector requires attention. For I-O purposes, the capital stock is usually expressed in the form of a capital-capacity output ratio, where capacity output represents the value of gross output given full capital stock utilization per year. The calculation of capacity output besides entailing some subtle theoretical difficulties, also requires some basic data on capacity utilization.[11] Unfortunately, the Soviet's have provided us with neither capacity output, nor capital utilization data, so that Soviet capital-output coefficients fail to conform to the desired capacity output standard. Instead, Soviet capital-output ratios refer to what might be called the adjusted, observed output criterion. Initially, Soviet capital stock data is found in capital/gross output form. Gross output, however, differs from the measure of total product flows utilized in our study in two ways. First, we employ the notion of gross domestic instead of gross output, subtracting imports from the latter.[12] Second we adjust gross domestic product by removing a portion of the turnover tax levied on commodities in the final demand matrix.[13] To make our treatment of capital coefficients consistent with product flows, we therefore transform the given Soviet capital-output ratios to an adjusted, gross domestic output basis. Consistency, however, does not bring us to the capacity output standard, so that our capital coefficients will fall short of the ideal to the extent that a portion of the capital stock remains idle. Just how serious this source of error may be cannot be ascertained.[14]

Labor coefficients derived from the original I-O employment data base were first published in 1965.[15] They refer to man years per 10,000 rubles of gross output and like the capital coefficients have been transformed to an adjusted gross domestic output basis, net of certain turnover taxes.[16] Unlike the capital coefficients, however, the labor coefficients are consistent with standard I-O practice.

Turnover taxes, profits, and subsidies are all of great interest to students of the Soviet economy. As we already noted these elements of value added were computed from standard sources and the 20 percent industrial sample. However, they do not appear as separate vectors in the 1959 table, but are aggregated into a heterogenous entity called other net income, thus greatly reducing the value of this potentially very useful information.

This brief examination of the data sources and data quality of quadrant III shows that it is composed of vectors with very different degrees of reliability. In fact, for our purposes, excluding imports which we shall comment on momentarily, only the capital, employment, and labor skills vectors are sufficiently dependable to merit our confidence.

No information on quadrant IV has yet been published.

E. Foreign Trade

Foreign trade poses a very special problem because the Soviets have never published input-output vectors of exports and imports. To fill in this gap in the I-O table recourse has been made to official Soviet foreign trade statistics published in substantial detail since 1955 in *Vneshniaia Torgovlia*. This makeshift approach has several weaknesses. First, the classification system used for the official foreign trade statistics are not always consistent with input-output vector nomenclature. Second, official foreign trade statistics are valued in foreign trade ruble prices, which are supposedly akin to international dollar values, instead of domestic prices. Since the 1959 I-O table is constructed in domestic prices, exports and import vectors valued in foreign trade ruble prices distort the tabular flow of actual physical quantities and are therefore inconsistent with the domestically valued portion of the table. Third is the more familiar problem of re-exports which are counted as both imports and exports in Soviet statistics. The consequence of such re-exports is to distort the real share of certain sectors in total Soviet exports and imports. The magnitude of this distortion is unknown, but another associated problem regarding the computation of the $(I-A)^{-1}$ matrix is easily disposed of, that is, the effect of re-exports on the computation of net exports. Equation (2.1) shows that in this case re-exports cancel each other out.

$$X - M = X + x' - (M + x') = X - M \tag{2.1}$$

where:

X = exports

M = imports

x' = re-exports

Of the three problems just discussed, the second is the most serious. Fortunately, it can be dealt with, though not in an altogether satisfactory way. In

1965, Efimov published export and import figures in domestic rubles for three large aggregates, producer goods, consumer goods, and agricultural products.[17] Treml took the Efimov data, and the official foreign trade figures aggregated according to the Efimov classification and formed conversion coefficients for each category linking domestic and foreign trade rubles. With the aid of these coefficients he was then able to obtain a rough estimate of the domestic value of imports and exports in each sector by inflating the appropriate official foreign trade figures. It must be openly acknowledged that the crudeness of the foreign trade data adjustment could lead to serious distortion in individual sectors. Just how seriously such distortions might affect our ultimate results will depend on the specific error distribution and cannot be judged a priori. The Efimov conversion coefficients have certainly improved the meaningfulness of the foreign trade I-O vectors, but their crudeness should be taken as another cautionary caveat when interpreting the final results of this study.

F. Prices

The Soviet input-output table is valued in purchasers' prices, which represent the actual prices paid to the supplier by the purchaser. Prices, however, are not invariant to the specific purchaser. In actual practice, prices are differentiated in very complex ways among a large number of identifiably different purchasers. For example, enterprises participating in the production process constitute a distinguishable purchaser type as opposed to private consumers who operate as purchasers of final goods. The price of an identical commodity will in general differ for intermediate and final purchasers through the mechanism of turnover taxes and subsidies. This means that the value flows represented in the input-output table will not accurately correspond to respective flows of physical goods. Moreover, purchasers' prices further distort true physical flows because they include transport costs which are already accounted for in the transportation sector. The Soviets were aware of this difficulty, but did not have sufficient information at their disposal to correct this defect through the use of producers' prices computed net of transport costs.[18] The substitution of producers' prices for purchasers' prices, however, still would not eliminate turnover tax and other price distortions. Ideally, if production potential were our concern, adjusted factor cost prices would be required. Needless to say we do not possess sufficient information to convert flows in purchasers' prices to flows based on the adjusted factor cost standard. A second best solution would require the elimination of turnover tax and the adoption of a one price criterion for identical goods consumed by intermediate and final purchasers. In the next chapter we will detail a crude adjustment technique utilized to attain this end.

G. Conceptual Problems

We will have occasion in this study to compare U.S. and U.S.S.R. factor proportions and therefore it is necessary to point out a special peculiarity of the Soviet input-output table, namely that the sectors are classified according to the gross social product concept. This means that all services not directly aiding material production are included with final demand rather than with inter-sectoral flows. Thus, passenger transportation, communications serving the nonproductive sphere, education, health and sanitary services, administration, financial and credit institutions, and defense, which are all classified as nonproductive, appear accordingly only in the second quadrant. The potential consequence on factor proportions of converting the Soviet I-O table to the American definition of productive activities cannot be measured, although we could adjust the U.S. table to conform to the gross social product standard. In this study we will have occasion to rely on an input-output study made by Robert Baldwin on a gross domestic product basis, so that the reader should bear in mind that classification factors may in part influence the observed results.

H. Treml's Recomputation

All of the foregoing discussion has centered on assessing the data underlying the construction of the Soviet input-output table in order to evaluate its overall reliability. Now a further complication must be noted. The Soviet input-output table has never been published in its entirety. Instead, a truncated 73 sector segment of the transactions matrix appeared in the 1960 edition of *Narodnaia Khozyaistvo SSSR*. Some of the ten missing vectors were actually aggregated into the published 73 sector matrix, but other vectors were totally omitted for security reasons. Through a combined approach of combing Soviet publications for the missing data, and estimating the omitted components for which supplementary data could not be obtained, Treml was able to produce a reconstructed version of the Soviet 1959 input-output table which appears reasonably consistent, with various tests of consistency performed by Treml—all of which showed the reconstructed table to be acceptably accurate. A detailed description of these tests can be found in Treml's technical paper, *The 1959 Soviet Intersectoral Flow Table.*[19]

As good as Treml's reconstruction undoubtedly is, it does take us one remove from the original table and therefore detracts from the table's overall reliability. Nevertheless, despite all its debilities, the Soviet 1959 input-output table seems to be sufficiently well constructed to justify the analysis to be undertaken in this study, provided the reader realizes the tentative nature of the results, which can in the future be scrutinized anew as more and better information becomes available.

Several reconstructed tables have been produced. The 66 square matrix has been chosen for our factor proportions study, representing as it does the most disaggregated version of the 1959 Soviet I-O table available.

3

The Embodied Factor Proportions Computation

A. The Leontief Statistic in Matrix Notation

An input-output table can be represented by a series of linear equations expressing the n sector utilization of n given outputs including final consumption.

$$a_{i1}x_1 + a_{i2}x_2 + \ldots + a_{in}x_n + c_i = x_i \qquad (3.1)$$

Equation (3.1) expresses this concept for any output x_i, $i = i(1, \ldots, n)$. The fixed technology and fixed input proportions assumptions characteristic of input-output methodology are expressed by the direct input coefficients a_{ij}, $i = i(1, \ldots, n)$, $j = j(1, \ldots, n)$. The x_j, $j = j(1, \ldots, n)$ variables represent the various sectors utilizing some portion of x_i given by the direct input coefficients a_{ij}, while c_i represents the share of x_i going to final consumption.

In general, an input-output table will be composed of n linear equations of the type shown in Equation (3.1). The entire set of such equations can be summarized in standard matrix form as

$$(I - A)X = C \qquad (3.2)$$

where:
I = an identity matrix
A = a matrix of the direct input coefficients a_{ij}
X = a matrix of output vectors
C = a matrix of final demand

If we desire to determine the total output required to sustain a given level of final demand, Equation (3.2) can be written as follows:

$$X = (I - A)^{-1} C \qquad (3.3)$$

where $(I - A)^{-1}$ stands for the Leontief inverse matrix, which represents the full input requirements, both direct and indirect, needed to produce the desired final demand bundle.

Knowledge of direct and indirect input requirements is crucial to the determination of factor proportions. As we noted in Chapter 2, Section D, direct capital coefficients are defined as the value of capital stock required to produce a unit of adjusted gross domestic output net of certain turnover taxes per year, while the direct labor coefficients relate to employment in 10,000 man years per ruble of adjusted gross domestic output, also net of certain turnover taxes. If we designate the direct capital coefficient vector by b and the direct labor coefficient vector by d, then the full, direct-plus-indirect factor requirements can be computed as follows:

$$k = b(I - A)^{-1} \tag{3.4}$$

$$l = d(I - A)^{-1} \tag{3.5}$$

where k represents the capital stock and l the man years required to deliver one unit of each sector's product to final demand.

Having determined the full factor requirements per unit delivery to final demand, factor proportions can readily be computed by multiplying vectors of import competing replacement goods (m) and exports (v) representing a proportional million rubles of each, by k and l to form the Leontief Statistic Ω

$$\Omega = \frac{km/lm}{kv/lv} \tag{3.6}$$

Equation (3.6) shows the Leontief Statistic where normalized import competing replacement goods and exports refer to commodity flows between the U.S.S.R. and the rest of the world. Leontief Statistics can also be computed for bilateral exchanges between the U.S.S.R. and specific individual countries, or bloc aggregates of individual countries. Sixty-two such bilateral Leontief Statistics have been computed for our study as follows:

$$\Omega_j = \frac{km_j/lm_j}{kv_j/lv_j} \qquad\qquad j = j \ (1, \ldots, 62) \tag{3.7}$$

where j stands for the index of the jth country, or BLOC aggregate. Thus, including the Leontief Statistic for U.S.S.R.-WORLD exchange 62 Ω's have been generated for use in our analysis of Soviet factor proportions. In addition, we have calculated factor proportions statistics for six labor skill vectors representing the disaggregated components of the labor vector. Sixty-two skill proportions statistics Θ were computed for each of the six primary labor skills giving us another 372 factor proportions statistics.

$$\Theta_{ij} = \frac{s_i m_j/lm_j}{s_i v_j/lv_j} \qquad\qquad i = i \ (1, \ldots, 6)$$
$$j = j \ (1, \ldots, 62) \tag{3.8}$$

Equation (3.8) expresses the skill factor proportions statistic in terms of a skilled labor-labor ratio where the i index denotes the six labor skills, and the j index the 62 bilateral units studied. Additional factor proportion statistics can readily be generated by taking ratios of one skill factor proportions statistic to another, or to the Leontief Statistic

$$\psi_{ijk} = \Theta_{ij}/\Theta_{kj} \qquad\qquad k = k \ (1, \ldots, 6) \qquad (3.9)$$
$$= \frac{s_i m_j / s_k m_j}{s_i v_j / s_k v_j} \qquad\qquad \begin{aligned} i &= i \ (1, \ldots, 6) \\ j &= j \ (1, \ldots, 62) \\ i &\neq k \end{aligned}$$

$$\phi_{ij} = \Omega_{ij}/\Theta_{ij} \qquad\qquad \begin{aligned} i &= i \ (1, \ldots, 6) \qquad (3.10) \\ j &= j \ (1, \ldots, 62) \end{aligned}$$
$$= \frac{k m_j / s_i m_j}{k v_j / s_i v_j}$$

Factor proportions statistics of this type have been used in regression analysis but are not otherwise analyzed in this book.

The discussion above has presented the standard procedure for the computation of the factor proportions statistics. It has been tacitly assumed that the input-output table used in that calculation was appropriately adjusted to correspond with certain important theoretical considerations commonly encountered in the literature. Our 1959 Soviet input-output table, however, does not conform with these theoretical canons so that it is necessary to explicitly detail the adjustments undertaken to put the original data in correct form.

B. Gross Domestic Product

The series of n equations described in Equation (2.1) can be put into the matrix form of Equation (3.11)

$$AX + C = X \qquad\qquad (3.11)$$

The term X on the right hand side of the equation corresponds to the notion of total gross output. It is, however, usually considered preferable to work with total gross domestic output because imports which are listed in the third quadrant, but really enter into production and consumption, are not taken account of in total gross output. By subtracting imports from exports we obtain a measure of total gross domestic output with all consumption accounted for. The adjustment required is the simple subtraction of the import vector from the export vector component of C which yields

$$A^*X^* + C^* = X^* \tag{3.12}$$

where:

X^* = gross domestic output, and $X^* < X$ by the amount $Z = C - C^*$

A^* = the new set of direct input coefficients

C^* = final consumption net of imports

C. Turnover Tax Adjustment

We mentioned in our discussion of input-output prices in Chapter 3 that a crude attempt would be made to correct the I-O data for turnover taxes and subsidies. To best appreciate the effect of turnover taxes on Soviet input-output value flows compare the matrix form of Equation (3.1) for a three sector model, with two types of final consumption, with all turnover taxes removed,

$$\begin{bmatrix} a_{11} & a_{12} & a_{13} \\ a_{21} & a_{22} & a_{23} \\ a_{31} & a_{32} & a_{33} \end{bmatrix} \begin{bmatrix} x_1 \\ x_2 \\ x_3 \end{bmatrix} + \begin{bmatrix} c_1 \\ & c_2 \\ & & c_3 \end{bmatrix} \begin{bmatrix} a_{14} & a_{15} \\ a_{24} & a_{25} \\ a_{34} & a_{35} \end{bmatrix} \begin{bmatrix} x_1 \\ x_2 \\ x_3 \end{bmatrix} = \begin{bmatrix} x_1 \\ x_2 \\ x_3 \end{bmatrix} \tag{3.13}$$

where:

$a_{i1}, \ldots, a_{i3}; i = i\ (1, \ldots, 3)$ are a set of technology coefficients

$a_{i4}, a_{i5}; i = i\ (1, \ldots, 3)$ are a set of coefficients specifying the share of final consumption in each sector going to the first and second final use

$x_i, i = i\ (1, \ldots, 3)$ are sectoral gross outputs

$c_i, i = i\ (1, \ldots, 3)$ equals the net output of each sector delivered to final demand

with the case where all turnover taxes are included

$$\begin{bmatrix} \lambda_{11}a_{11} & \lambda_{12}a_{12} & \lambda_{13}a_{13} \\ \lambda_{21}a_{21} & \lambda_{22}a_{22} & \lambda_{23}a_{23} \\ \lambda_{31}a_{31} & \lambda_{32}a_{32} & \lambda_{33}a_{33} \end{bmatrix} \begin{bmatrix} x_1 \\ x_2 \\ x_3 \end{bmatrix} + \begin{bmatrix} c_1 \\ & c_2 \\ & & c_3 \end{bmatrix} \tag{3.14}$$

$$\begin{bmatrix} \lambda_{14}a_{14} & \lambda_{15}a_{15} \\ \lambda_{24}a_{24} & \lambda_{25}a_{25} \\ \lambda_{34}a_{34} & \lambda_{35}a_{35} \end{bmatrix} = \begin{bmatrix} \lambda_1 x_1 \\ \lambda_2 x_2 \\ \lambda_3 x_3 \end{bmatrix}$$

Taking any row over all three matrices, the second for example,

$$\lambda_{21}a_{21}x_1 + \lambda_{22}a_{22}x_2 + \lambda_{23}a_{23}x_3 + \lambda_{24}c_{21} + \lambda_{25}c_{22} = \lambda_2 x_2 \qquad (3.15)$$

we observe that the turnover tax levied on goods produced in the second sector varies by purchasing sector. In general $\lambda_{2i} \neq \lambda_{2j}$, where λ_{ij} is the turnover tax paid for the ith commodity purchased by the jth sector. For our purposes it is convenient to define the turnover tax coefficient λ_{ij} as $\lambda_{ij} = 1 + n_{ij}$, where n_{ij} is the increment of nominal value added to $a_{ij}x_i$ due to the turnover tax charge. The right side of Equation (3.15) exceeds its pre-tax counterpart by the aggregate turnover tax coefficient λ_2, which represents the sum of all λ_{2j}, $j = j(1, \ldots, 5)$ turnover tax levies, weighted by the share of each purchasing sector $x_{2j}/x_j = w_{2j}$ including final demand in the total product of sector 2. Since λ_2 conceptually includes all turnover tax, to account for indirect tax resulting from tax levies on sectors 2's inputs we interpret λ_{22} in Equation (3.15) as a coefficient representing tax on own use λ_{22} and the sum of all indirect turnover tax charges τ_2.

$$\lambda_2 = \sum_{j=1}^{5} \lambda_{2j} w_{2j} \qquad (3.16)$$

Likewise, in the case of the remaining sectors turnover taxes will distort the real value of commodity flows and in addition the average incidence of turnover will vary since for any two sectors λ_i will not in general equal λ_j, so that Equation (3.14) differs from (3.13) in two ways. First, the rate of turnover tax incidence on the output of any sector will vary with each particular purchasing sector, and second, the average rate of turnover tax levied on the output of any sector, say the ith, will differ from that levied on any other jth sector. Clearly then, to adequately adjust Equation (3.14) to (3.13) we require knowledge of all λ_{ij}'s, which can then be removed by elementary row or column operations.

The requisite λ_{ij} data, however, is unavailable, and therefore in practice turnover tax adjustment requires some simplifying assumptions. First, we assume that there exist two basic turnover tax rates for every sector's output, an average rate levied on intermediate uses λ_i, $i = i(1, \ldots, n)$, and an average rate on goods delivered to final output μ_i, $i = i(1, \ldots, m)$; and second that on average the turnover tax levied on the final goods of each sector exceeds the analogous levy on intermediate goods, so that $\mu_i > \lambda_i$, where $\mu_i = \epsilon_i \lambda_i$ and $\epsilon_i = (1 + \gamma_i)$, γ_i, $i = i(1, \ldots, n)$, representing turnover tax increment by which μ_i exceeds the basic λ_i charge. In addition it should be noted that the taxes charged to productive inputs of any sector x_j are included in the value of final x_j output, so that in evaluating turnover tax distortion both direct and indirect turnover tax effects should be borne in mind. Given these simplifying assumptions we can rewrite Equation (3.14) with the aid of three diagonal turnover tax matrices

$$\begin{bmatrix} \lambda_1 & & \\ & \lambda_2 & \\ & & \lambda_3 \end{bmatrix} \begin{bmatrix} a_{11} & a_{12} & a_{13} \\ a_{21} & a_{22} & a_{23} \\ a_{31} & a_{32} & a_{33} \end{bmatrix} \begin{bmatrix} x_1 \\ x_2 \\ x_3 \end{bmatrix} + \tag{3.17}$$

$$\begin{bmatrix} \mu_1 & & \\ & \mu_2 & \\ & & \mu_3 \end{bmatrix} \begin{bmatrix} c_1 & & \\ & c_2 & \\ & & c_3 \end{bmatrix} \begin{bmatrix} a_{14} & a_{15} \\ a_{24} & a_{25} \\ a_{34} & a_{35} \end{bmatrix} =$$

$$\begin{bmatrix} \delta_1 & & \\ & \delta_2 & \\ & & \delta_3 \end{bmatrix} \begin{bmatrix} x_1 \\ x_2 \\ x_3 \end{bmatrix}$$

where each δ_i, $i = i(1, \ldots, 3)$ turnover tax rate represents the average of the two average turnover taxes λ_i and μ_i paid by purchasers of the ith commodity and weighted respectively by the share of intermediate and final goods in total gross sectoral output.

$$\delta_i = \sum_{j=1}^{3} \lambda_{ij} x_{ij}/x_i + \sum_{j=1}^{2} \mu_{ij} x_{ij}/x_i \tag{3.18}$$

Our goal as before remains the elimination of all turnover tax. If we could find two diagonal inverse matrices Λ^{-1}, and M^{-1} we could achieve this objective by multiplication with the diagonal matrices Λ and M.

$$\Lambda\Lambda^{-1} A_{11} X + MM^{-1} CA_{12} = \tag{3.19}$$

$$IA_{11} X + ICA_{12} =$$

$$A_{11} X + CA_{12} = X$$

where A_{11} is the matrix of technology and A_{12} the matrix of final demand coefficients.

Soviet data, however, is again inadequate in this regard, so that we must abandon any hope of transforming Equation (3.17) into the turnover tax free form (3.19). However, a third best possibility remains. If we could obtain information on the relationship between average intermediate and average final product turnover taxes we could deflate the final product turnover taxes to the intermediate product rates even though we lack direct knowledge of the magnitude of the intermediate turnover tax rates themselves. For example, assuming as we have, in line with Soviet practice, that $M = (1 + \Gamma)\Lambda$, where $\Gamma > 0$ and M, Λ and $(1 + \Gamma)$ are diagonal matrices, if we can obtain information directly on $(1 + \Gamma)$, then we can premultiply the M matrix in Equation (3.17) by $(1 + \Gamma)^{-1}$ to obtain final demand valued in prices gross of turnover tax levied at intermediate goods rates alone.

$$
\begin{bmatrix} \dfrac{\lambda_1}{\mu_1} & & \\ & \dfrac{\lambda_2}{\mu_2} & \\ & & \dfrac{\lambda_3}{\mu_3} \end{bmatrix}
\begin{bmatrix} \mu_1 & & \\ & \mu_2 & \\ & & \mu_3 \end{bmatrix}
\begin{bmatrix} c_1 & & \\ & c_2 & \\ & & c_3 \end{bmatrix}
\tag{3.20}
$$

$$
\begin{bmatrix} a_{14} & a_{15} \\ a_{24} & a_{25} \\ a_{34} & a_{35} \end{bmatrix}
=
\begin{bmatrix} \lambda_1 & & \\ & \lambda_2 & \\ & & \lambda_3 \end{bmatrix}
\begin{bmatrix} c_1 & & \\ & c_2 & \\ & & c_3 \end{bmatrix}
$$

$$
\begin{bmatrix} a_{14} & a_{15} \\ a_{24} & a_{25} \\ a_{34} & a_{35} \end{bmatrix}
=
\begin{bmatrix} \lambda_1 c_1 a_{14} & \lambda_1 c_1 a_{15} \\ \lambda_2 c_2 a_{24} & \lambda_2 c_2 a_{25} \\ \lambda_3 c_3 a_{34} & \lambda_3 c_3 a_{35} \end{bmatrix}
\qquad \textbf{1793091}
$$

Although this transformation fails to eliminate total turnover tax distortion, it succeeds in achieving two desirable results. First, it removes a portion, and in the Soviet case the preponderant portion (72 percent) of all turnover tax levied on gross output. Second, and perhaps of equal importance, transformation of final into intermediate turnover tax rates allows us to value the commodity flow matrices consistently in prices gross of intermediate turnover taxes, so that a rubles worth of output in the intersectoral flow matrix is equivalent to a rubles worth of output in the final demand matrix

$$
\begin{bmatrix} \lambda_1 & & \\ & \lambda_2 & \\ & & \lambda_3 \end{bmatrix}
\begin{bmatrix} a_{11} & a_{12} & a_{13} \\ a_{21} & a_{22} & a_{23} \\ a_{31} & a_{32} & a_{33} \end{bmatrix}
\begin{bmatrix} x_1 \\ x_2 \\ x_3 \end{bmatrix}
+
\tag{3.21}
$$

$$
\begin{bmatrix} \lambda_1 & & \\ & \lambda_2 & \\ & & \lambda_3 \end{bmatrix}
\begin{bmatrix} c_1 & & \\ & c_2 & \\ & & c_3 \end{bmatrix}
\begin{bmatrix} a_{14} & a_{15} \\ a_{24} & a_{25} \\ a_{34} & a_{35} \end{bmatrix}
=
$$

$$\begin{bmatrix} \lambda_1 & & \\ & \lambda_2 & \\ & & \lambda_3 \end{bmatrix} \begin{bmatrix} x_1 \\ x_2 \\ x_3 \end{bmatrix}$$

Fortunately we do possess Soviet data which allows us to estimate the $(1 + \Gamma)^{-1}$ matrix, so that equation (3.21) represents the actual form in which the Soviet input-output table is valued for the purposes of this study.

Information on the $(1 + \Gamma)^{-1}$ matrix comes from foreign trade statistics. We mentioned earlier that, using Efimov's indices of domestic import and export ruble purchaser values, Treml had computed a series of coefficients which were essentially exchange rates between domestic rubles in purchasers' prices and foreign trade rubles for specific commodity aggregates: producers' goods, consumers' goods and agricultural products. These coefficients are shown in Table 3.1 where it is apparent that import and export goods in the same classification are valued in intermediate purchasers' prices net of direct turnover tax, but including turnover tax paid by the producing sector on its inputs.[1] Imports, on the other hand are valued in final purchasers' prices including turnover tax levied at rates applicable to final consumers. This means using our simplifying turnover tax structure assumptions that exports are valued according to Equation (3.22)

$$\begin{bmatrix} \lambda_1 & & \\ & \lambda_2 & \\ & & \lambda_3 \end{bmatrix} \begin{bmatrix} v_1 & & \\ & v_2 & \\ & & v_3 \end{bmatrix} = \begin{bmatrix} \lambda_1 v_1 & & \\ & \lambda_2 v_2 & \\ & & \lambda_3 v_3 \end{bmatrix} \tag{3.22}$$

and imports according to Equation (3.23)

$$\begin{bmatrix} \mu_1 & & \\ & \mu_2 & \\ & & \mu_3 \end{bmatrix} \begin{bmatrix} m_1 & & \\ & m_2 & \\ & & m_3 \end{bmatrix} = \begin{bmatrix} \mu_1 m_1 & & \\ & \mu_2 m_2 & \\ & & \mu_3 m_3 \end{bmatrix} \tag{3.23}$$

Table 3-1
Purchasing Power Parity Ratios of Soviet Producers', Consumers' and Agricultural Goods, Using Domestic/Foreign Trade Ruble Prices

	Imports	Exports
Producers' Goods	1.07	1.12
Consumers' Goods	3.44	1.67
Agricultural Goods	4.17	1.32

Now if imports and exports of each sectoral classification constitute similar bundles of goods, that is, if $M \approx V$, then premultiplying the right side of Equation (3.22) by the inverse of the right side of (3.23) we obtain an approximation of the $(1 + \Gamma)^{-1}$ matrix.[2]

$$
\begin{bmatrix}
\dfrac{1}{\mu_1 m_1} & & \\
& \dfrac{1}{\mu_2 m_2} & \\
& & \dfrac{1}{\mu_3 m_3}
\end{bmatrix}
\begin{bmatrix}
\lambda_1 v_1 & & \\
& \lambda_2 v_2 & \\
& & \lambda_3 v_3
\end{bmatrix}
\approx
\tag{3.24}
$$

$$
\begin{bmatrix}
\dfrac{\lambda_1}{\mu_1} & & \\
& \dfrac{\lambda_2}{\mu_2} & \\
& & \dfrac{\lambda_3}{\mu_3}
\end{bmatrix}
=
\begin{bmatrix}
1+\gamma_1 & & \\
& 1+\gamma_2 & \\
& & 1+\gamma_3
\end{bmatrix}
$$

It should be understood that our estimated $(1 + \Gamma)^{-1}$ matrix suffers from two shortcomings. First, the commodity composition of a unit of output from a given producing sector delivered to imports and exports might differ, $m_i \neq v_i$ for the same aggregate good x_i. This problem of course is endemic to deliveries to all using sectors in I-O tables and an estimation of its potential significance cannot be made with the data at hand. Second, since the Soviet I-O table contains 66 producing sectors, to properly transform the final demand turnover tax diagonal matrix M we require 66 $(1 + \gamma)^{-1}$ diagonal elements, one for each producing sector. Each $(1 + \gamma_i)^{-1}$ element should reflect the ratio of intermediate to final turnover tax rates for each specific sector. Soviet turnover tax conversion coefficients derived from 3.2n however relate to the average ratio of intermediate to final turnover tax rates for three large aggregates: producers', consumers' and agricultural goods, so that our estimated $(1 + \Gamma)^{-1}$ matrix will diverge from the true one wherever the specific sector turnover tax conversion coefficient diverges from the relevant aggregate average. As we admitted at the outset, our turnover tax deflation procedure is crude, but it should nonetheless substantially reduce the aggregate turnover tax distortion in the final demand matrix, where the preponderant portion of total turnover taxes are levied, while at the same time making the unit value of commodity flows consistent with unit physical flow through the table.

Three additional matters related to turnover tax require mention at this point. First, imports which are shown as a row vector in the third quadrant of the Soviet I-O table were transposed and deflated in the same manner as the rest of the final demand matrix, so that imports are consistently valued with first and second quadrant flows.

$$
\begin{bmatrix} \dfrac{\lambda_1}{\mu_1} & & \\ & \dfrac{\lambda_2}{\mu_2} & \\ & & \dfrac{\lambda_3}{\mu_3} \end{bmatrix} \begin{bmatrix} \mu_1 & & \\ & \mu_2 & \\ & & \mu_3 \end{bmatrix} \begin{bmatrix} m_1 \\ m_2 \\ m_3 \end{bmatrix} = \begin{bmatrix} \lambda_1 m_1 \\ \lambda_2 m_2 \\ \lambda_3 m_3 \end{bmatrix} \tag{3.25}
$$

Second, the denominator of the direct capital and labor coefficients, gross outputs, has been adjusted to the gross domestic output definition and μ turnover taxes removed to yield gross domestic output inclusive of λ turnover taxes

$$
\begin{bmatrix} \lambda_1 x_1 \\ \lambda_2 x_2 \\ \lambda_3 x_3 \end{bmatrix} \tag{3.26}
$$

where the intermediate turnover tax rates include on our assumptions both direct and indirect turnover tax, since deflation of the final demand matrix does not remove indirect charges. Once again, therefore, the I-O data is valued consistently gross of turnover taxes levied at intermediate good rates.

Finally, it should be noted that the capital stock itself is valued with prices gross of turnover taxes levied at appropriate intermediate product rates, which however can be characterized as negligible.[3] Thus, in sum, our turnover tax adjustment procedure has been applied consistently to all elements of the Soviet I-O data.

D. Import Competing Goods

In computing the Leontief Statistic we made one additional adjustment to the 1959 Soviet input-output table that merits special comment. Factor proportions analysis compels us to work with import competing replacement goods rather than imports, because the factor requirements of noncompetitive import replacements could be extraordinarily great, and thereby distort the Leontief Statistic. In the U.S. input-output table imports are partitioned into two vectors, one for competitive and the other for noncompetitive imports. This makes the proper proportioning of competitive import replacements a trivial matter. In the Soviet case on the other hand, the task of defining our own vector of noncompetitive imports had to be faced. It was assumed that the Soviets were capable of producing all the industrial goods they imported. This narrowed the task down to ascertaining the agricultural commodities which could not be grown within the boundaries of the U.S.S.R., primarily: coffee, cocoa, spices, cashew nuts, and jute. Using the classification utilized by Treml in the construction of the input-output table, the first four items were treated as food (sector 59) while jute was categorized as a textile (sector 56). It should be noted that two items, tea and bananas, which appear as noncompetitive imports in the U.S. I-O table are competitive in the Soviet Union. In fact 4 percent of the world output of tea is produced in the U.S.S.R.

Having identified noncompetitive imports, it is a simple matter to subtract these noncompeting import goods from total imports for all the countries studied and the world as a whole. To evaluate the magnitude of the adjustment for noncompetitive imports it is sufficient to note that in 1959 noncompetitive food imports comprised 13 percent, and textile imports 1 percent of the total imports of their respective sectors.

These then are the major adjustments undertaken in the computation of the Soviet Leontief Statistic. We are now ready to analyze the results of our computations.

Part II
Soviet Factor Proportions:
Empirical Results

4

The Neoclassical Factor Proportions of Soviet International Trade 1955–1968

In the foregoing chapters we have discussed the theoretical foundations of factor proportions analysis, explained the computational procedures utilized in the measurement of Soviet factor proportions and evaluated the accuracy of the data underlying the factor proportions calculation. We are now almost ready to present our findings and analyze their significance, but before we begin it is necessary to say a few words concerning the measurement of the Soviet Leontief Statistic which as we have already explained is a ratio of two ratios, the numerator representing the direct-plus-indirect ratio of capital to labor embodied in a proportioned million rubles' worth of import competing replacement goods, and the denominator representing the same measure for exports.[1]

$$\Omega = \frac{km/lm}{kv/lv} \tag{4.1}$$

Factor proportions neutrality is defined as

$$km/lm = kv/lv \tag{4.2}$$

which implies that the Leontief Statistic Ω is precisely equal to one. If the embodied capital-labor ratio computed for imports and exports should be unequal a nonneutral bias emerges. When the numerator exceeds the denominator we speak of a capital intensive import bias; when the reverse situation obtains, a capital intensive export bias. As the Leontief Statistic stands, a capital intensive import bias is measured on a scale from the neutral point one to infinity, whereas the capital intensive export bias is measured over the domain one to zero. This means that bias values greater than one are scaled numerically, while bias values less than one are measured on an inverse numerical scale. Since a capital intensive import bias is distinguished from a capital intensive export bias solely on the basis of the national origin of the underlying commodities, this asymmetricity in the measurement of the factor proportions bias can be a source of palpable distortion. To remedy this deficiency, we have in our graphical analysis rescaled the Leontief Statistic on a consistent and symmetric numerical basis, by setting the factor proportions neutral point equal to zero, measuring the capital intensive export bias in terms of negative deviations, and the capital intensive import bias in terms of positive deviations from zero. Negative bias is computed as: $-\left(\frac{1}{\Omega} - 1\right)$. In rescaling the Leontief Statistic it was necessary to change the factor proportions neutrality point from one to zero in order to make the ordering continuous. Defining the bias in terms of positive or negative deviations about the number 1 would have resulted in a downward semicontinuous scale with a gap between the values one and minus one.

In the sections that follow we will present the traditional Leontief values in statistical tables, but in measuring factor proportions bias and conducting graphical analysis we shall rely on rescaled Leontief values. This procedure, it is hoped, will facilitate comparison with other Leontief Statistic studies and at the same time enable us to handle capital intensive import and export biases symmetrically in our analysis.

A. Leontief Statistics Generated in U.S.S.R.-WORLD International Commodity Exchange

It is well known that each time the Leontief Statistic has been computed for the United States, the results have shown a strong capital intensive import bias.[2] For the years 1947, 1951, and 1962 the American Leontief Statistics were respectively 1.2996, 1.0577 and 1.27.[3] Table 4.1 presents analogous Soviet Leontief Statistics for the years 1955, 1959, 1963, and 1968. These figures are graphed in Figure 4-1. along with the American Leontief Statistics to facilitate comparison. Both statistical and graphical presentations bring out some striking contrasts between American and Soviet factor proportions. First, the value of the American Leontief Statistic exceeds the Soviet's in every case, which implies that the capital intensive import bias is always less, or the capital intensive export bias is always greater in U.S.S.R.-WORLD than in U.S.-WORLD inter-

Table 4-1
The Soviet Leontief Statistics Generated in U.S.S.R.-World Trade Compared With Analogously Defined American Leontief Statistics

Year	Leontief Statistics	
	U.S.S.R.	U.S.A.
1947		1.2996
1951		1.0577
1955	1.0288	
1959	0.9244	
1962		1.27
1963	0.8051	
1968	0.7142	
1957-1962		1.2091
1955-1968	0.8681	

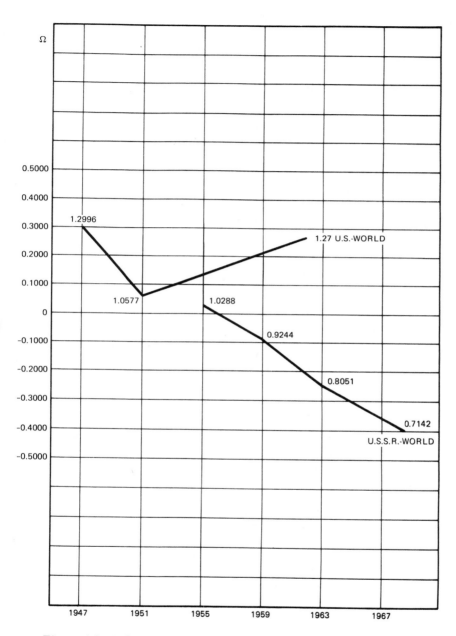

Figure 4-1. A Comparison of American and Soviet Leontief Statistics Generated in U.S.-WORLD and U.S.S.R.-WORLD Trade over the Period 1947-1968.

national commodity exchange. Second, in only one year, 1955, do we find the Soviet Leontief Statistic exceeding one. In all other years the Soviets export relatively capital intensive and import relatively labor intensive goods, in the absolute sense that the Leontief Statistic is less than one. Third, we discover that the Soviet Leontief Statistic is a monotonically decreasing function of time, declining at a remarkably regular rate. The measurement of this trend, however, presents a problem because of the bias reversal in 1959. To overcome this awkward measurement difficulty we introduce the notion of a "bias unit," defined as a 10 percent deviation in either direction from the factor proportions neutrality point zero, where the Leontief Statistic is measured on the symmetric, continuous numeric scale discussed earlier. Applying the "bias unit" concept we find that the Soviet Leontief Statistic declined 4.29 bias units over the entire period 1955-1968, or at a rate of 1.07 bias units per observation. In contrast, the U.S. Leontief Statistic does not manifest a clear-cut trend.

In evaluating the behavior of the Soviet Leontief Statistic it is important to realize that the same 1959 Leontief inverse matrix is used in the computation of Soviet factor proportions for all the years listed in Table 4-1. The Soviet Leontief Statistic for each year is computed as follows:

$$\Omega_i = \frac{k_{59}m_i/l_{59}m_i}{k_{59}v_i/l_{59}v_i} \tag{4.3}$$

where the subscript i refers to the proportioned import or export bundle of the ith year, and the subscript 59 refers to full factor requirements given the 1959 Leontief inverse and factor structure. With the per ruble direct-plus-indirect factor requirements being held constant, it is evident that the increasing capital intensity of Soviet exports over time is caused solely by the changed commodity structure of imports and exports. Changes in the structure of the technology matrix, therefore, do not account for any part of the observed results. An analysis of intertemporal changes in the commodity structure of Soviet international trade will be undertaken in Chapters 7. For the moment we need only recognize that the most salient characteristics of the U.S.S.R.-WORLD Soviet Leontief Statistics are their capital intensive export bias, and the regularity of the secular trend towards the increased capital intensity of the export bias. Overall, the contrast between U.S. and U.S.S.R. Leontief Statistics is most strikingly revealed in summary form by the U.S. average rescaled value of 0.2091 and the Soviet figure of minus 0.1519, which reflect the central factor proportions tendencies of both countries: the strong capital intensive import bias in the U.S. and the more modest capital intensive export bias in the U.S.S.R.

B. Soviet Leontief Statistics Generated in U.S.S.R.-CMEA Trade[4]

The commodity structure of Soviet international trade is sharply differentiated by regional trade blocs. Since factor proportions are linked directly with commodity structure, we should anticipate that Leontief Statistics associated with the various U.S.S.R.-REGIONAL commodity structures will differ both among themselves and from U.S.S.R.-WORLD results. To assess this hypothesis let us look first at Table 4-2, which presents the Leontief Statistics computed for trade between the Soviet Union and the Council for Mutual Economic Assistance, the CMEA. Table 4-2 is divided into two segments. The first row refers to U.S.S.R.-CMEA trade as a whole, while the remaining rows give the Soviet

Table 4-2
Soviet Leontief Statistics[a] Generated in Trade Between the U.S.S.R. and the CMEA[b] for the Years 1955, 1959, 1963, 1968

U.S.S.R. Trade Pattern With	Soviet Leontief Statistics Year				
	1955	1959	1963	1968	1955-1968
1. CMEA and its components	1.3478	1.0626	0.8106	0.6967	0.9794
2. Czechoslovakia	2.2758	1.2087	0.9902	0.8472	1.3305
3. East Germany	1.5437	1.3556	0.9607	0.9878	1.2120
4. Hungary	0.8384	0.7025	0.5955	0.5886	0.6813
5. Poland	1.0783	1.1999	0.9184	0.7530	0.9874
6. Rumania	1.0776	0.7912	0.5805	0.5499	0.7498
7. Bulgaria	0.7069	0.6099	0.5597	0.4434	0.5800

[a]The general formula for Soviet Leontief Statistics computed for U.S.S.R.-REGIONAL, or U.S.S.R.-COUNTRY trade is

$$(4.4) \qquad \Omega_{ij} = \frac{k_{59}m_{ij}/l_{59}m_{ij}}{k_{59}v_{ij}/l_{59}v_{ij}} \qquad \begin{array}{l} j=j\,(1,\ldots,61) \\ i=i\,(1,\ldots,4) \end{array}$$

where:

k = direct-plus-indirect capital requirements per ruble of sector output
l = direct-plus-indirect labor requirements per 10,000 man years per ruble of sectoral output
m = import competing replacement goods
v = exports
i = the year index
j = the country or regional index

[b]Only the European members of the CMEA, excluding Albania, are included in this study.

Leontief Statistic for U.S.S.R.-COUNTRY exchange with each CMEA member taken separately. To facilitate the reader's comprehension a rescaled graphical presentation of U.S.S.R.-CMEA Leontief Statistics is also supplied in Figures 4-2 and 4-3, to supplement the tabular material.

Let us begin by first considering Table 4-2, row 1 and Figure 4-2. In 1955 we find that U.S.S.R.-CMEA exchange is characterized by a substantial capital intensive import bias, equivalent to 3.48 bias units. This figure stands in sharp contrast to the U.S.S.R.-WORLD capital intensive import bias of 0.29 bias units. Between 1955 and 1959 the capital intensive import bias declines 82 percent from 3.48 to 0.63 bias units, but this sharp decrease is insufficient to cause a factor bias reversal, which means that in 1959 U.S.S.R. factor proportions were capital intensive *export biased* over all in U.S.S.R.-WORLD trade, but capital intensive *import biased* in trade with the socialist bloc. However, by 1963 not only do we find that a factor proportions reversal has occurred in U.S.S.R.-CMEA trade, but that the magnitude of the resulting capital intensive export bias almost exactly approximates the U.S.S.R.-WORLD capital intensive export bias. Moreover, despite an obvious abatement in the rate of increase in the capital intensity of the U.S.S.R.-CMEA export bias, the Leontief Statistic generated in Soviet trade with the CMEA continues to fall more rapidly than the average U.S.S.R.-WORLD rate, with the result that by 1968 for the first time the magnitude of the U.S.S.R.-CMEA capital intensive export bias surpasses that produced in U.S.S.R.-WORLD exchange, reaching a level of minus 4.28 bias units.

If we examine the shift in factor proportions in U.S.S.R.-WORLD and U.S.S.R.-CMEA trade over the entire period 1955-1958 we find that the U.S.S.R.-CMEA Leontief Statistic declined 7.76 bias units in contrast to 4.29 for U.S.S.R.-WORLD trade, or at a rate 1.8 times faster than the economy-wide average. However, the fact that the rate of decline in the capital intensity of the U.S.S.R.-CMEA export bias is sharply reduced from 1963-1968 suggests that it would be unwise to project these differential rates of decline in the Soviet Leontief Statistic into the future.

A disaggregation of the U.S.S.R.-CMEA Leontief Statistics into their component parts reveals that the Soviet Union in its trade with all six CMEA member states manifested a secular tendency towards increased capital intensive exports, but the pattern and rates of increase differed widely among Russia's socialist bloc trading partners, as can be seen in Figure 4-3. Soviet trade with four of the six CMEA member states, Czechoslovakia, East Germany, Poland, and Rumania, demonstrates factor proportions bias reversal at some time between 1955 and 1968, while Soviet exchange with two BLOC countries, Hungary and Bulgaria, is consistently capital intensive export biased. Regarding the magnitude of capital intensive export bias two distinct groupings are discernible: Czechoslovakia, East Germany, and Poland on one hand, Hungary, Rumania, and Bulgaria on the

49

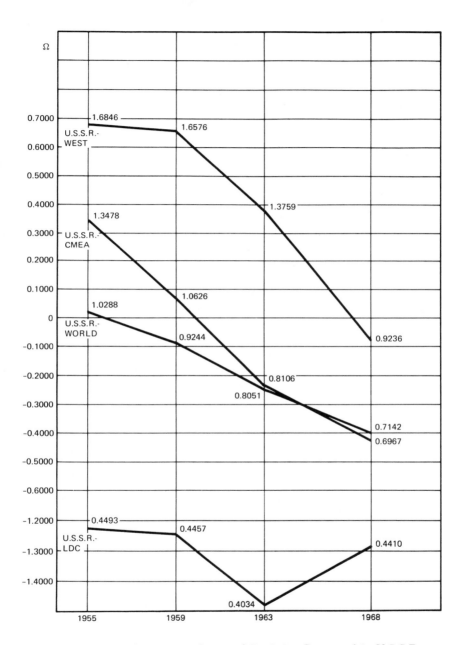

Figure 4-2. Trends in Soviet Leontief Statistics Generated in U.S.S.R.-
WEST, U.S.S.R.-CMEA, and U.S.S.R.-LDC Trade Over the Period
1955-1968.

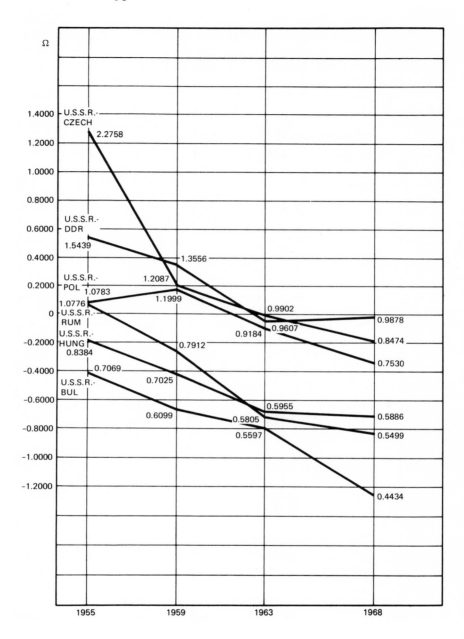

Figure 4-3. Trends in Soviet Leontief Statistics Generated in Trade With Six Member States of the CMEA Over the Period 1955-1968.

other. Soviet trade with the first division is on average substantially less capital intensive in exports, with U.S.S.R.-Czechoslovakian and U.S.S.R.-East German Leontief Statistics manifesting an overall capital intensive import bias. Although the two groups tend to reflect differences in per capita GNP, a fully correct ordering on this basis would require transferring Hungary to the first and Poland to the second grouping.

In addition to general differences in the profile and time patterns of Soviet Leontief Statistics generated in Russian trade with each CMEA member state, the rates of change in factor proportions bias also differ in important ways. U.S.S.R.-East German, U.S.S.R.-Hungarian, and U.S.S.R.-Polish factor proportion biases shift towards increased capital intensity in exports at a 27 percent slower $(1 - \frac{4.87}{7.76})$ pace than the all U.S.S.R.-CMEA average of 7.76 bias units, while U.S.S.R.-Rumanian and U.S.S.R.-Bulgarian Leontief Statistics decrease 12 percent $(\frac{8.69}{7.76}$ bias units) faster than the U.S.S.R.-CMEA average. However only in U.S.S.R.-Czechoslovakian exchange, where a 14.56 bias unit shift represents a rate of capital intensification in exports almost twice as fast as the U.S.S.R.-CMEA trend, is there a substantial difference in intra-CMEA Leontief Statistic rate of change over the period 1955-1968.

Taking all these variations in the pattern and rate of factor proportions change into consideration for each U.S.S.R.-CMEA member pairing, it is hard to escape the conclusion that the overall U.S.S.R.-CMEA constitutes a fair summary statistic of all these individual trends. Thus disaggregation of the U.S.S.R.-CMEA composite demonstrates that not only are U.S.S.R.-CMEA Leontief Statistics characterized by a strong secular trend towards an increasingly capital intensive export bias, but with surprising consistency each of the CMEA member states manifests, with slight modification, the same basic secular trend. An important corollary of this result is that each and every CMEA member state, as well as the CMEA as a whole, in its trade with the Soviet Union exhibits a declining trend in its Soviet Leontief Statistic values that is more rapid than the U.S.S.R.-WORLD rate.

C. Soviet Leontief Statistics Generated in U.S.S.R.-WEST Trade[5]

Turning to the U.S.S.R.-WEST case, an inspection of Table 4-3 and Figure 4-2 immediately reveals, that with due allowance for individual vagaries, the pattern of Leontief Statistics generated in Soviet trade with the WEST taken as a unit is remarkably similar to U.S.S.R.-CMEA factor proportions structure. U.S.S.R.-WEST Leontief Statistics, it is true, start from a much more capital intensive import biased position (6.84 bias units) and end with a higher capital intensive export bias, but disregarding differences of overall level, they hold many

Table 4-3

Soviet Leontief Statistics for Trade Between the U.S.S.R. and the WEST[a] in the Years 1955, 1959, 1963, 1968

U.S.S.R. Trade Pattern With	Soviet Leontief Statistic Year				
	1955	1959	1963	1968	1955-1968
1. WEST and its components	1.6846	1.6576	1.3759	0.9236	1.4400
2. United Kingdom	2.0284	1.8933	1.9432	1.3312	1.3968
3. West Germany	1.8387	1.4931	1.1158	0.8929	1.3352
4. France	1.1144	1.3944	1.2759	0.8805	1.1663
5. Finland	1.6566	1.5464	1.2554	0.6887	1.2868

[a]WEST is defined as the United Kingdom, West Germany, France, and Finland which on average 1955-1968 account for 53 percent of Soviet trade with developed capitalist countries.

important properties in common. First, like the U.S.S.R.-CMEA case, Soviet trade with the WEST starts with a labor intensive export bias and terminates in a modest capital intensive export bias (0.83 bias units). Only a single four year time period separates the U.S.S.R.-CMEA and U.S.S.R.-WEST factor bias reversals, and even this time difference appears to reflect the differential magnitude of the starting point more than anything else. Second, the rates of decline in the capital intensity of the export biases East and West are very similar. Over the entire thirteen year time span 1955-1968 U.S.S.R.-WEST factor proportions changes 7.67 bias units, or at a rate almost identical to the one encountered in the U.S.S.R.-CMEA case. Thus there is palpable evidence suggesting that some common causal nexus underlies the factor proportions pattern of Soviet trade not just with the CMEA, but with the developed world as a whole.[6]

Furthermore, if we extend our analysis further to the U.S.S.R.-COUNTRY level Figure 4-4 shows that on the whole the factor proportions structure generated in Soviet trade with the WEST taken as a unit, is a fairly faithful rendering of the factor proportions pattern characterizing Soviet trade with each of the member states of the WEST aggregate taken individually. All four countries in their trade with the U.S.S.R. manifest secularly declining capital intensive export biases. In the cases of U.S.S.R.-France, U.S.S.R.-West German, and U.S.S.R.-Finnish trade this secular decline culminates in 1968 in factor reversals of substantial proportion. Only U.S.S.R.-British trade fails to produce a factor reversal. But even in this case a clear tendency towards an eventual reversal is evidenced by the fact that in the thirteen years from 1955 to 1968 the capital intensity of the U.S.S.R.-British export bias fell 6.97 bias units, or 1.5 times the average U.S.S.R.-WORLD rate. Regarding the rate structure of the

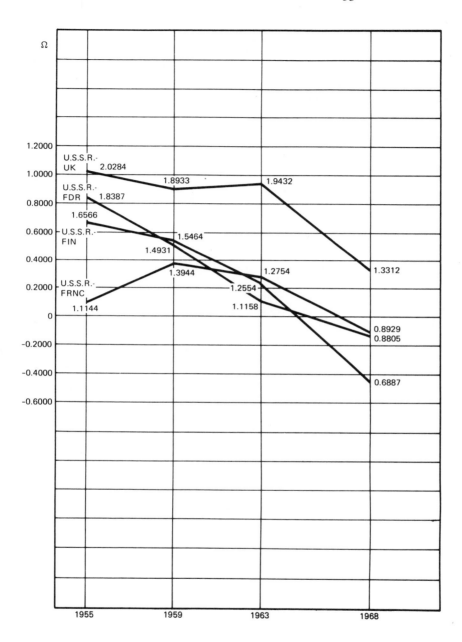

Figure 4-4. Trends in U.S.S.R.-WEST Soviet Leontief Statistics for Four Individual Western Countries Over the Period 1955-1968.

secularly declining Leontief Statistic trend in the other U.S.S.R.-COUNTRY cases we find a somewhat dispersed pattern. The U.S.S.R.-French trend falls only 2.7 bias units, or 0.68 bias units per observation, while at the other extreme the U.S.S.R.-West German and U.S.S.R.-Finnish trends decline at rates of 2.4 and 2.8 bias units per period. This rate spread notwithstanding, the sum force of the evidence at hand suggests that the secularly declining capital intensive export bias trend encompasses Soviet trade with all developed countries viewed either as BLOC aggregations or taken individually, which is a very powerful finding.

D. Soviet Leontief Statistics Generated in U.S.S.R.-LDC Commodity Exchange[7]

Factor proportions generated in Soviet bilateral commodity exchange with the less developed countries aggregate composed of China, India, and the United Arab Republic provide important information necessary for a complete understanding of U.S.S.R.-WORLD factor proportions. We noted earlier that U.S.S.R.-CMEA and U.S.S.R.-WEST Leontief Statistics were higher than U.S.S.R.-WORLD values for 1955 and 1959. Table 4-4 and Figure 4-2 show that Soviet Leontief Statistics generated in trade with the LDC, which accounts for 33 percent of the total Soviet trade in these years, readily explain this phenomenon by revealing that U.S.S.R.-LDC factor proportions are characterized by a capital intensive export bias of 12.23 in 1955 and 12.24 bias units in 1959. Biases of this dimension are encountered in Soviet bilateral commodity exchange with individual Western countries, but not with the WEST or CMEA aggregates themselves. They appear not only to account for the greater than average Soviet Leontief Statistic values in U.S.S.R.-WEST and U.S.S.R.-CMEA trade, but to explain why even in the 1950s the Soviet Union, which by every measure is less capital rich than the United States, exhibits a capital intensive *export bias* in its

Table 4-4

Soviet Leontief Statistics Generated in Bilateral U.S.S.R.-LDC Commodity Exchange

U.S.S.R. Trade Pattern With	Soviet Leontief Statistics Year				
	1955	1959	1963	1968	1955-1968
1. LDC and its components	0.4493	0.4457	0.4034	0.4410	0.4349
2. United Arab Republic	0.3031	0.4567	0.3628	0.4884	0.4045
3. China	0.4542	0.4494	0.4192	0.3526	0.4188
4. India	0.3432	0.3552	0.3695	0.4034	0.3678

trade with the world as a whole, when U.S.-WORLD trade manifests a capital intensive *import bias*. If we consider the time trend of U.S.S.R.-LDC factor proportion values, Table 4-4 shows little ostensible change; however, the rescaled numeric index indicates that the Leontief Statistic for 1963 evidences a sharp downward break in an otherwise stable trend.[8] The increase in the capital intensity of the export bias between 1959 and 1963 is 2.35 bias units, but in 1968 it is offset by a decrease in the capital intensity of the export bias of 2.12 bias units, so that it is impossible to argue that U.S.S.R.-LDC commodity exchange is characterized by the secular trend towards an increasingly capital intensive export bias noted for U.S.S.R.-CMEA and U.S.S.R.-WEST factor proportions. Disaggregating the less developed countries unit into its component parts we find in Table 4-4 and Figure 4-5 that the underlying pattern of Soviet bilateral factor proportions with China, India, and the UAR taken individually is quite erratic. The U.S.S.R.-UAR value in particular is extremely unstable, fluctuating 11.10 bias units between 1955 and 1959, 5.12 from 1959-1963, and 6.59 from 1963-1968. U.S.S.R.-CHINA factor proportions exhibit a secular trend towards an increasingly capital intensive export bias with its Leontief Statistics declining 6.34 bias units from 1955-68, while over the same time horizon, factor proportions expressing bilateral Soviet commodity exchange with India manifest the opposite tendency, showing a secularly decreasing capital intensive export of 4.35 bias units. The extreme diversity in these trends mirrors the heterogeneity of the LDC aggregate and the special role that political considerations play in Soviet trade with developing countries. Nevertheless, the aggregate of these disparate trends appears to furnish us with a reasonable overall picture of factor proportions in U.S.S.R.-LDC trade as a whole, reflecting a stable intertemporal bilateral U.S.S.R.-LDC factor proportion pattern. The single exception here is the 1963 U.S.S.R.-LDC Leontief Statistic displays a sharp decline due to the impact of the 5.12 bias unit decline in U.S.S.R.-UAR exchange. However, judging by the fact that the U.S.S.R.-WORLD trend is apparently unperturbed by this sharp rise in the capital intensity of the Soviet export bias with the less developed countries, changes in the factor proportions generated in Soviet trade with other unsampled elements of the developing nations as well as changes in bilateral trade imbalances not adequately reflected in the standard Leontief-type computation probably have an offsetting impact on the U.S.S.R.-LDC Leontief Statistic encompassing all less developed nations. If this interpretation is correct, it means that Soviet factor proportions characteristic of U.S.S.R.-LDC trade should properly be viewed as exhibiting a constant trend between 1955-1968, so that in sum our analysis of U.S.S.R.-LDC Leontief Statistics demonstrates that Soviet commodity exchange with the less developed countries explains not only the direction of the U.S.S.R.-WORLD capital intensity bias in the 1950s, but the relatively slow secular trend towards an increasingly capital intensive export bias displayed in U.S.S.R.-WORLD trade, in comparison with the rates of decline manifested in U.S.S.R.-CMEA and

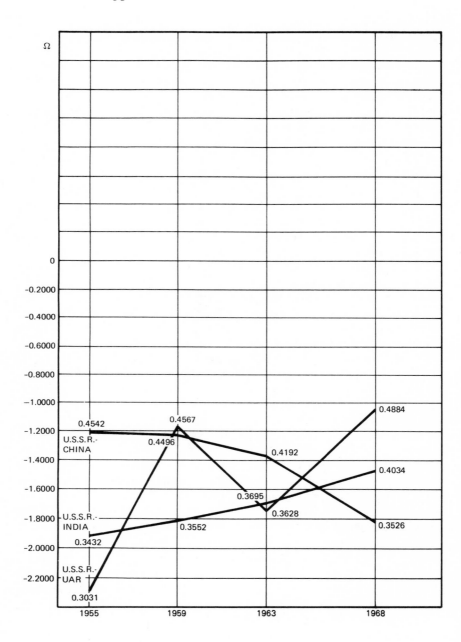

Figure 4-5. Trends in U.S.S.R.-CHINA, U.S.S.R.-INDIA and U.S.S.R.-UAR Leontief Statistics 1955-1968.

U.S.S.R.-WEST exchange. These summary observations are important in themselves and for the analysis as a whole, because they show that the structures of Soviet bilateral Leontief Statistics with the WORLD, is consistent with the pattern of Soviet Leontief Statistics of its component parts.

One further remark is in order. We argued earlier that trends in the value of Soviet Leontief Statistics demonstrated a common pattern for Soviet bilateral trade with the developed nations as a whole. Our survey of the factor proportions structure of U.S.S.R.-LDC exchange indicates that a distinctly different set of forces are at work in Soviet trade with the developed and less developed nations. In Chapter 7, Section C however, we will demonstrate that this is not an entirely correct deduction.

E. A Method for the Evaluation of the Compatibility of Soviet Leontief Statistics and the Heckscher-Ohlin Theorem I

In Chapter 1, section C, we argued that the Heckscher-Ohlin theorem should be logically decomposed into two parts, the first emphasizing the tendency for relative international factor availabilities to determine the structure of international commodity flows, and the second stressing the notion of full factor price equalization. We labeled the first hypothesis Heckscher-Ohlin I and asserted that factor availabilities should exert an important influence on the structure of commodity flows even under Soviet socialism. Given the nature of Soviet planning, we also argued that the second Heckscher-Ohlin theorem predicting full factor price equalization was even more unrealistic under Soviet than under Western conditions, and therefore we would focus our analysis on Theorem I. It is now time to ascertain whether the commodity structure of Soviet international trade does in fact reflect the influence of underlying factor availabilities.

To test the hypothesis that Soviet Leontief Statistics are generated according to the principles embodied in the first Heckscher-Ohlin theorem we need to demonstrate that there exists a correlation between the factor availability ratios of the Soviet Union's trading partners and the value of the Soviet Leontief Statistic.

$$\Omega = \phi\left(\frac{K}{L}\right) \qquad (4.4)$$

where:

Ω = the Soviet Leontief Statistic

$\frac{K}{L}$ = the capital-labor ratio.

If the trading partner is capital rich vis-à-vis the U.S.S.R. we would anticipate high values for the Soviet Leontief Statistic reflecting the importation of capital intensive and the exportation of labor intensive commodities. Where the trading partner is labor rich, the reverse result would be expected. Since the Heckscher-Ohlin theorem I emphasizes only a tendency for factor availabilities to determine the pattern of commodity flows, as support for the conjecture we might anticipate a scatter of observations similar to the one depicted in Figure 4-6. Soviet Leontief Statistics are arrayed on the vertical and the capital-labor ratio on the horizontal axis. Points in quadrant I, where the Leontief Statistic is greater than or equal to one, should correspond to cases in which the trading partner of the U.S.S.R. is characterized by a capital-labor ratio greater than the Soviet's, while points in quadrant III should be associated with countries whose capital-labor ratio is lower than the Soviet's. Given consistent numerical scaling a random scatter of observations in Figure 4-6 would falsify the contention that

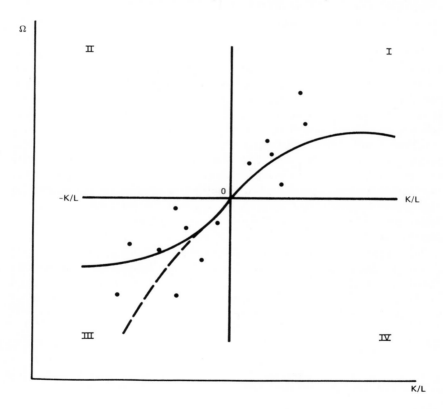

Figure 4-6. Hypothetical Scatter Diagram Illustrating the Association Between Soviet Leontief Statistics and the Capital-Labor Ratio.

Soviet Leontief Statistics are generated in accordance with the laws of Heck-scher-Ohlin theory. On the other hand a tight, positively sloped linear scatter passing through the hypothetical U.S.S.R.-U.S.S.R. point at zero would suggest that Soviet Leontief Statistics are very strongly influenced by relative factor availabilities and conform to a linear specification.[9] In evaluating the plausibility of a linear specification, it must be remembered that the capital-labor variable refers to foreign factor proportions. There is no bar in principle to the Soviet Leontief Statistic being a linear function of the foreign capital-labor ratio, where as Heckscher-Ohlin theory requires production functions are internationally identical, linear homogeneous and in addition permit factor substitution. But the mechanics of the input-output computation make this outcome unlikely. The fixed input proportions assumption of input-output analysis places a lower and an upper bound on domestic factor intensity for any import competing output structure. As the gap between foreign and domestic factor proportions increases changes in the value of Ω will reflect this divergence progressively less completely, until in the limit where all import competing goods are concentrated in the Soviet's most capital, or most labor intensive activity, Ω will attain its maximum or minimum boundary value. Thus, while the linear specification is probably accurate over a limited range around the Soviet capital labor value, outliners will likely have a less than proportional, as well as a diminishing impact on Ω. Geometrically the anticipated behavioral relationship between Ω and K/L is best described by the hyperbolic tangent function depicted in Figure 4-6. This specification, however, is only accurate if the capital-labor ratio is rescaled in accordance with the symmetricity convention applied to Ω, a procedure which raises severe difficulties in subsequent regression studies. To avoid these problems it has proven expedient to preserve the traditional scaling for the factor proportions variable.[10] As a consequence of this scaling decision the hyperbolic tangent form is modified insofar as the inverse of the K/L ratio approaches infinity at a much more rapid rate than the negative range of Ω measured along the ordinate. The resulting curve whose tail is indicated by the dashed line in Figure 4-6 is semi-logarithmic, and it is this specification that we would anticipate observing if all the requisite data were at hand. Algebraically, therefore, we desire to test the expression

$$\Omega = \gamma + \beta \log K/L \qquad (4.5)$$

where Ω = a vector of Soviet Leontief Statistics

γ = a constant

$\dfrac{K}{L}$ = a vector of capital-labor ratio values

β = the coefficient of the capital-labor ratio

Although as we shall see the semi-logarithmic specification produces the best econometric fit for the observed data, comparative regression results for the linear form using asymmetrically scaled variables also have high explanatory value. For those who might prefer the linear specification comparative econometric evidence is provided where appropriate.

In attempting to implement this test of the relationship between the Soviet Leontief Statistic and the Heckscher-Ohlin theorem I, we require information on capital and labor availabilities of all the Soviet Union's trading partners for which we have computed Leontief Statistics. Unfortunately capital stock data of the type required is unavailable so that we need an instrumental variable which is correlated with factor availabilities in order to analyze the theoretical importance of our Leontief Statistics. The variable chosen as our factor availabilities proxy is per capita gross national product. The use of this variable can be justified on the rather loose ground that differences in national income levels among countries are positively correlated with differences in capital formation. If labor is assumed internationally homogeneous, and differences in natural resource endowments and technology are positively associated with capital formation levels, then international differences in per capita GNP can be attributed solely to capital formation. These are sweeping assumptions. The argument that natural resource endowments and capital formation are correlated is particularly poor. This is strikingly evident for hole-in-the-ground economies like Kuwait, which fortuitously do not enter into our analysis. Furthermore, GNP levels may reflect productive efficiency as well as factor availabilities. Nevertheless, I feel there exists a common-sense presumption, particularly for the countries selected in our study, that international differences in per capita national income are positively correlated with differences in domestic capital stock or capital availabilities.

The selection of per capita GNP as our factor availabilities proxy does not however settle the question of the nature of the functional relationship linking per capita GNP and the capital-labor ratio. One plausible approach would be to conjecture that all the economies under consideration can be characterized by Cobb-Douglas aggregate production functions:

$$Y = AK^\tau L^{1-\tau} \tag{4.6}$$

If we convert Equation (4.6) to a per capita basis

$$\frac{Y}{L} = \frac{AK^\tau L^{(1-\tau)}}{L^\tau L^{(1-\tau)}} = A\left(\frac{K}{L}\right)^\tau \tag{4.7}$$

we find that per capita GNP is a nonlinear function of the capital labor ratio and the technology coefficient A. Moreover, by taking logs of both sides of the equation we obtain a linear relationship between the suggested per capita GNP instrumental variable and the capital-labor ratio.

$$\log \frac{Y}{L} = \log A + \tau \log \frac{K}{L} \tag{4.8}$$

The advantage of this specification of the functional form of the relationship between per capita GNP and capital-labor availabilities is that it conforms with modern neoclassical thinking regarding aggregate production functions. In particular, it embodies the notion of diminishing marginal productivity of a variable factor when an ancillary input is held constant. A linear specification does not possess this property. However, to accurately adjust each per capita GNP value at the very least we would require information concerning the τ value for every Soviet trading partner. Since such information is unavailable, as a second best we can estimate an average multi-national τ indirectly by postulating a semi-log relationship between the rescaled Soviet Leontief Statistic and per capita GNP.

Assume that per capita GNP is a multi-national Cobb-Douglas function of capital and labor. By rearranging terms in Equation 4.8 we can solve for the capital-labor ratio in terms of per capita income.

$$\log \frac{K}{L} = \frac{1}{\tau} \log \frac{Y}{L} - \frac{1}{\tau} \log A \tag{4.9}$$

Substituting the right hand side of Equation 4.9 into Equation 4.5 we obtain

$$\Omega = \frac{\beta}{\tau} \log \frac{Y}{L} + (\gamma - \frac{\beta}{\tau} \log A) \tag{4.10}$$

Letting $\beta^* = \dfrac{\beta}{\tau}$ and $\eta = \gamma - \dfrac{\beta}{\tau} \log A$ we find

$$\Omega = \eta + \beta^* \log \frac{Y}{L} \tag{4.11}$$

which specifies the rescaled Soviet Leontief Statistic as a semi-logarithmic function of per capita GNP and an amalgamated constant term. By regressing the log of per capita GNP on the Soviet Leontief Statistic we can obtain a coefficient β^* which includes the average multi-national Cobb-Douglas coefficient τ.

The discovery of a good fit for Equation 4.11 has several interesting implications. First, it demonstrates that the Soviet Leontief Statistic is a hyperbolic tangent function of symmetrically normalized capital-labor availabilities in accordance with our discussion of the underlying structural specification. Second, we establish that the multi-national Cobb-Douglas function, with its important and reasonable property of diminishing marginal productivity to increases in per capita capital formation, is consistent with our empirical findings. The function is not necessarily Cobb-Douglas because not knowing β independently of τ, τ may be > 1, or < 0. Notice, however, that whether the function is or is not Cobb-Douglas the diminishing marginal productivity property is preserved. Finally, it is easy to demonstrate that if our results are consistent with the Cobb-Douglas specification, as they appear to be, they will also be compatible with any other linear homogeneous form including CES and VES specifications. These properties taken together with graphical evidence showing our observations falling in quadrants I and III and the semi-log regression line passing through the U.S.S.R.-U.S.S.R. trade point constitute formidable evidence in favor of the hypothesis that Soviet Leontief Statistics are consistent with the Heckscher-Ohlin theorem. We shall now demonstrate that Soviet Leontief Statistics possess these precise properties.[11]

F. The Empirical Relationship Between Soviet Leontief Statistics and Per Capita Gross National Product

Figures 4-7—4-9 detail the relationship between various subsets of Soviet Leontief Statistics and per capita GNP, our instrumental variable for capital-labor availabilities. The computation of a consistent set of per capita GNP statistics based on Milton Gilbert's purchasing power parity calculations for Western and Thad Alton's computations for East European countries is explained in Appendix A. The per capita GNP values employed in our figures refer to average values 1955-1968 in 1967 prices. Similarly, the Soviet Leontief Statistics represent average values for the same time period. The exact figures are presented in Tables 4-2—4-4. Average per capita GNP and Soviet Leontief Statistic values, rather than yearly figures, are used for both variables to eliminate fluctuations occurring in any specific year, and to remove the influence of the secular trend towards an increasing capital intensive bias in Soviet exports discussed in sections A-D.

We will have more to say about this secular trend in due course; for the moment, however, let us first consider the relationship between average Soviet Leontief Statistics and average per capita GNP. Figure 4-7 illustrates this relationship for trade between the U.S.S.R. and the thirteen countries selected for this study. Soviet Leontief Statistics are arrayed along the ordinate; per capita GNP along the abscissa. If we divide the figure into four quadrants by making the hypothetical observation of the U.S.S.R.-U.S.S.R. trade the origin of a set of coordinate axes, by inspection we find that countries with per capita GNPs less than the Soviet's all fall in the third quadrant, while those possessing per capita GNPs greater than the Soviet's fall entirely in the first quadrant. This result, in accordance with our discussion of Figure 4-6, clearly shows that there does exist a tendency for Soviet Leontief Statistics to be positively associated with our per

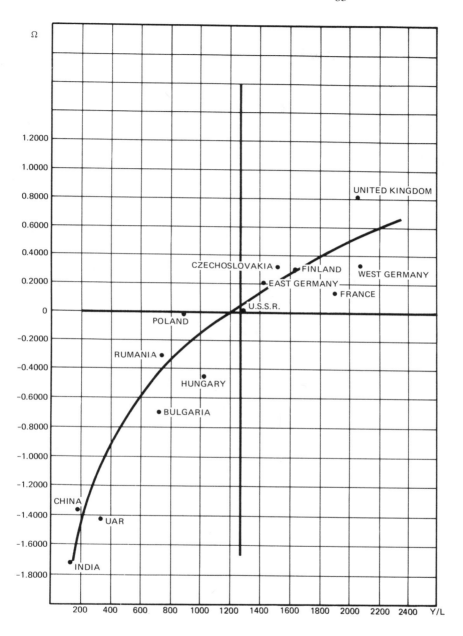

Figure 4-7. 1955-1968 Average Soviet Leontief Statistics Generated in Trade With 13 Countries, Plotted as a Function of Per Capita GNP.

capita GNP proxy for the capital-labor availabilities ratio. While the clustering of points in quadrants I and III in the scatter diagram (Figure 4-7) sufficiently demonstrates Soviet trade with the member states of the CMEA, WEST, and LDC divisions conform with the principles of Heckscher-Ohlin theorem I, it is equally evident that the semi-log specification of Equation (4.11) best describes the observed scatter. A semi-log regression run on all fourteen country observations, including the hypothetical U.S.S.R.-U.S.S.R. point, yields an R of 0.9615 with a β coefficient of 1.98004, significant at the 0.995 level. If we remember that our observations come from a cross-section study, rather than a time series, this semi-logarithmic fit, explaining 92.5 percent of the variance in the dependent variable, must be viewed as a very impressive indication of the basic conformity of Soviet factor proportions with the laws of Heckscher-Ohlin theorem I.[12] This conclusion is further buttressed by noting in Figure 4-7 that the semi-logarithmic regression line passes very close to, if not through the U.S.S.R.-U.S.S.R. point, showing that there does not exist any unexplained cumulative capital intensive import or export bias. These are exceedingly important findings because they represent the fullest possible test of the Heckscher-Ohlin theorem under Soviet conditions prevailing over the period 1955-1968, using the traditional neoclassical inputs capital and labor. Not only do our results confirm the Heckscher-Ohlin consistency of Soviet factor proportions in trade with the countries studied, but the semi-logarithmic fit suggests first that our per capita GNP variable is consistent with a multi-national Cobb-Douglas production function, and second that the direct relationship between Soviet Leontief Statistics and capital-labor availabilities is hyperbolic tangential in accordance with the symmetric scaling convention utilized in Figure 4-6. These last two results attest significantly to the fact that the Heckscher-Ohlin theorem I consistency of our Soviet Leontief Statistics is not an aberration, but reflects valid underlying economic forces.

The strongly Heckscher-Ohlin theorem I rational results obtained thus far have been based on average values for Soviet Leontief Statistics and per capita GNP, 1955-1968. Insofar as the averaging process has tended to eliminate random fluctuations in these variables in any specific year the outcome has been to the good. But in our analysis of Tables 4-2–4-4 we detected a secular trend towards an increased capital intensive export bias in Soviet trade with the CMEA and the WEST. Since the averaging process conceals the impact of this secular trend, it is now necessary to discover what effect this secular trend has had first on the validity of the Heckscher-Ohlin theorem as an explanation of Soviet Leontief Statistic values and second on the functional form of the relationship between the observed Soviet Leontief Statistics and per capita GNP. We will endeavor to assess the consequence of the secular trend by examining the correlation between Soviet Leontief Statistics and per capita GNP in 1955 and 1968. The initial and terminal years of our study have been selected for special considera-

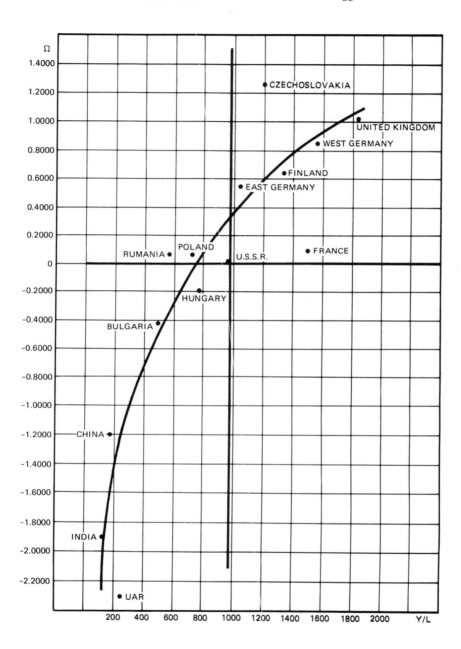

Figure 4-8. Soviet Leontief Statistics for 1955 Generated in Trade With 13 Countries, and Plotted Against 1955 Per Capita GNP.

tion because they demonstrate the maximum impact of the secular trend on the Soviet Leontief Statistics. Figure 4-8 illustrates the point scatter of Leontief Soviet Statistics and per capita GNP for the year 1955.[13] We note first, as might be expected, that the observations are obviously more widely dispersed than in Figure 4-7, due in part to random forces at work in any single year. Nevertheless a semi-log specification appears to fit the scatter reasonably well, although the slope is somewhat steeper than the gradient in Figure 4-7.[14] Secondly, we must observe that two points, one representing U.S.S.R.-Rumanian and the other U.S.S.R.-Polish trade fall in quadrant II. This indicates that the Soviet Leontief Statistics associated with these points are, contrary to Heckscher-Ohlin theorem I, negatively correlated with our capital-labor availabilities proxy. On the whole, however, the positive correlation required prevails with a slight tendency evident for the Soviet Leontief Statistics to exhibit labor intensive export biases somewhat greater than called for on the basis of Heckscher-Ohlin theorem I. Thus, the scatter Figure 4-8 shows that the averaging process for the initial year 1955 conceals a modest labor intensive export bias, but the functional form remains semi-logarithmic and broadly compatible with Figure 4-7.

When we turn our attention to the relationship between Soviet Leontief Statistics and per capita GNP in 1968, however, the situation is considerably altered. Figure 4-9 suggests that the functional form of the relationship between Soviet Leontief Statistics and per capita GNP is still semi-logarithmic,[15] but the regression locus now passes to the southeast of the U.S.S.R.-U.S.S.R. trade point indicating a secular capital intensive export bias, expressed as a parametric shift factor, in U.S.S.R.-CMEA and U.S.S.R.-WEST commodity trade. As a consequence of this secular trend five observations, all for the relatively developed nations of the group, fall in quadrant IV, showing a negative correlation between these Soviet Leontief Statistics and per capita GNP. In 1955 the negative correlation indicated a violation of the first Heckscher-Ohlin theorem with a bias to excessively labor intensive exports; in 1968, however, the negative correlation refers to a bias towards excessively capital intensive exports. Both the number of negatively correlated observations and the magnitude of their deviation from their correct location in quadrant I for the 1968 is greater than for 1955. If the secular trend displayed over the period 1955-1968 continues, we would anticipate that sometime in the near future the Soviet Union will demonstrate a capital intensive export bias in its trade with all countries. Some of these capital intensive export biased points, those in quadrant III, will be justified according to Heckscher-Ohlin theorem I, but the points in quadrant IV will violate the theorem even though a positively sloped semi-logarithmic curve adequately describes the functional relationship between the Soviet Leontief Statistics and the capital-labor availabilities proxy. Thus, Figures 4-8 and 4-9 taken together reveal that the averaging of the values of both variables 1955-1968 conceals a tendency for Soviet Leontief Statistics to be progressively less compatible with the principles of Heckscher-Ohlin theorem I, due to a secular trend towards an

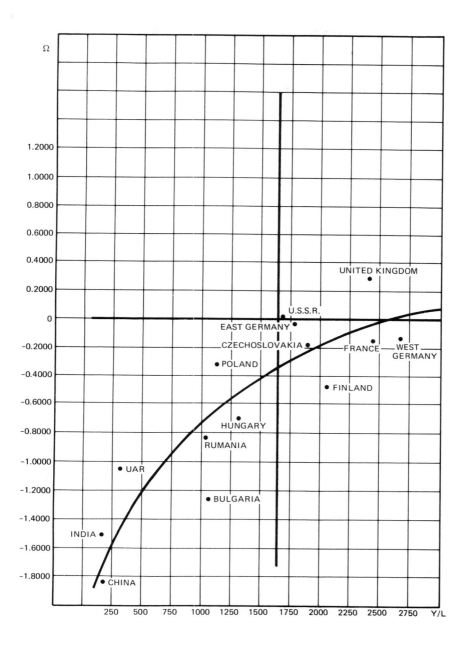

Figure 4-9. 1968 Soviet Leontief Statistics Generated in Trade With 13 Countries, Taken as a Function of 1968 Per Capita GNP.

overall capital intensive bias of Soviet exports with all trading partners, regardless of their level of economic development. Nevertheless, despite the excessive capital intensity of Soviet exports to the WEST and certain CMEA members, a positive, though weakening, semi-logarithmic correlation between Soviet Leontief Statistics and per capita GNP still persists showing that the factor availabilities of the U.S.S.R.'s trading partners is not altogether irrelevant.

Furthermore, it may still be possible to reconcile the secular trend toward an increased capital intensive export bias with Heckscher-Ohlin theorem I by noting that per capita GNP is only a proxy for capital-labor availabilities. If the ratio of capital-labor availabilities has increased more rapidly in the Soviet Union than elsewhere it is possible that many of the fourth quadrant observations actually belong in quadrant I. If we consider trends in net investment in the Soviet Union and the economies of its trading partners there is some evidence that this may be a partial explanation of the secular trend. Table 4-5 presents indices of net investment, population and the ratio of these two variables. The net investment indices are not completely compatible with the capital stock measure employed in the Soviet input-output table, differing primarily by the inclusion of housing and fixed asset formation in the service sector. Moreover, should depreciation rates differ internationally, our measure of fixed capital formation will be

Table 4-5
Indices of Net Investment and Population Growth for Ten Countries 1955-1968

Country	(I) Index of Net Investment	(L) Index of Population Growth	I/L
1. U.S.S.R.	286	121	236
2. United Kingdom	194	107	181
3. West Germany	201	114	176
4. France	288	114	253
5. Finland	173	110	157
6. Czechoslovakia	208	109	191
7. East Germany	339	96	353
8. Hungary	306	104	294
9. Poland	252	117	215
10. Bulgaria	701	111	632

Sources: Data for the U.S.S.R. comes from NARODNOYE KHOZYAISTVO SSSR V 1965, AND 1968 G. Soviet capital formation figures are gross. Information on net investment for CMEA countries is found in Thad Alton, "Economic Structure and Growth in Eastern Europe," ECONOMIC DEVELOPMENTS IN COUNTRIES OF EASTERN EUROPE, JEC, 1970, p. 53. East European population statistics were taken from Paul Myers, "Demographic Trends in Eastern Europe," ECONOMIC DEVELOPMENTS IN THE COUNTRIES OF EASTERN EUROPE, JEC, 1970, pp. 125-137. Data for the WEST all come from the NATIONAL ACCOUNTS OF THE OECD COUNTRIES, 1950-1968, OECD, Paris, 1970.

accordingly distorted. Nevertheless Table 4-5 should provide a rough approximation to the relative changes in capital-labor availabilities in the various countries considered over the time span 1955-1967. If we focus first on the member states of our WEST aggregate we find that the Soviet capital-labor ratio increased 23 percent more than the average increase of our four WEST countries. Using our dollar measures of per capita GNP, I calculated that per capita product increased 10 percent more in the Soviet Union than in the WEST. This means that our per capita GNP proxy does indeed understate the relative increase in capital-labor availabilities in the U.S.S.R. But the degree of understatement seems hardly to be of sufficient magnitude to account for the 5.23 bias unit decline 1955-1968 in the Soviet Leontief Statistic generated in trade between the U.S.S.R. and the WEST. This impression is reinforced when we consider relative capital-labor ratio changes between the U.S.S.R. and the CMEA. For a few cases, notably Czechoslovakia and Poland, the increased capital intensity bias of Soviet exports can in part be attributed to the more rapid increase of the capital-labor ratio in the Soviet Union. But U.S.S.R.-East German, U.S.S.R.-Hungarian, and U.S.S.R.-Bulgarian exchange also manifest sharply declining Soviet Leontief Statistic values despite the fact that the relative capital-labor ratio is increasing substantially faster in these countries than in the Soviet Union. When due consideration is given possible ambiguities and errors in the underlying data, it still seems clear that the secular trend towards an increased capital intensive bias in Soviet exports is only partially related to changes in underlying factor proportions consistent with Heckscher-Ohlin theorem I. Thus, while on average over the period 1955-1968 Soviet Leontief Statistics remarkably conform with the laws of Heckscher-Ohlin theorem I, a secular trend resulting in the progressive violation of these laws has been detected, which cannot be adequately explained by changes in factor availabilities in the various countries studied.

5

The Role of Third Factors and the Importance of Non-Neoclassical Factor Aggregates in the Determination of the Structure of Soviet Commodity Trade 1955-1968

Our analysis of Soviet factor proportions thus far has been founded on the assumption that neoclassical factor aggregates, capital-labor availabilities, best characterized the inputs determining the commodity structure of Soviet international trade. In this chapter we shall attempt to evaluate the merit of working with non-neoclassical factor aggregates under Soviet conditions. Two avenues will be explored in this regard. First, using the same basic data employed for the computation of Soviet Leontief Statistics in Chapter 4, we can delete the effect of certain key vectors in order to ascertain whether special factors in these sectors crucially influence the full 66 sector Soviet Leontief Statistic values. Second, we can explicitly compute Soviet Leontief Statistics using other factor proportions ratios. Data at hand permit us to study the following basic factor ratios:[1]

1. Skilled labor to average labor, where skilled labor is defined as administrative-managerial, supervisory, and engineering personnel with completed higher education
2. Secondary labor skills to average labor, where secondary labor skills are defined as other engineering and technical supervisory personnel.
3. Tertiary skilled labor to average labor, where tertiary skills are defined as workers employed in production or auxiliary services of the highest skill group.
4. Quaternary skilled labor to average labor, where quaternary skilled labor is defined as workers employed in production or auxiliary services with medium skills.
5. Unskilled labor to average labor.
6. Miscellaneous labor to average labor, where miscellaneous labor is defined as other employees including trainees, apprentices, clerical personnel, watchmen, etc.

In addition, various permutations of these six ratios, plus the capital variable, enable us to analyze an exceedingly large number of non-neoclassical factor proportions ratios at different levels of aggregation. To sort through the multitude of factor proportion sets at our disposal a search procedure utilizing a stepwise regression program was employed to locate the most promising factor proportion combinations. Although most factor proportions sets have some special interest, only the most theoretically attractive cases were selected for analysis in this chapter.

A. Soviet Leontief Statistics with the Influence of the Natural Resource Sectors Removed

Natural resources have been singled out for special consideration by students of factor proportions because they constitute a plausible unproduced third aggregate factor which can be utilized to explain the famous Leontief Paradox.[2] Jaroslav Vanek, by deleting the natural resource vectors from the computation of the Leontief Statistic showed that the Leontief Paradox was reversed. His theoretical explanation for this result was that capital and natural resources were complementary, causing the United States to exchange labor intensive commodities for capital-natural resource intensive goods.[3] William Travis and Vanek have both shown that this explanation is inconsistent with the Heckscher-Ohlin approach because if natural resources are the truly scarce factor in the U.S., America should exchange capital intensive for natural resource intensive goods.[4]

Table 5-1
Soviet Leontief Statistics Generated in Trade Between the U.S.S.R. and 13 Other Countries in the Years 1955, 1959, 1963, 1968 With the Natural Resources Vectors (1,3,8,9,11,51a) Deleted

U.S.S.R. Trade Pattern With	Soviet Leontief Statistics (60 Sectors) Year				
	1955	1959	1963	1968	1955-1968
1. WORLD	0.9718	0.9540	0.8977	0.8695	0.9233
2. WEST and its components	1.9008	2.0189	1.5928	1.2710	1.6959
3. United Kingdom	2.1419	2.2322	2.0902	1.3293	1.9484
4. West Germany	1.8785	1.7826	1.2729	1.2999	1.5285
5. France	1.7336	1.7889	1.5920	1.4068	1.6303
6. Finland	1.8054	1.9334	1.6203	1.1346	1.6234
7. CMEA and its components	1.3980	1.2064	0.9465	0.8253	1.0941
8. Czechoslovakia	2.0388	1.4509	1.3754	1.1238	1.4972
9. East Germany	1.8312	1.5664	1.1342	1.1733	1.3138
10. Hungary	0.9907	0.9910	0.7178	0.6262	0.8314
11. Poland	1.0237	1.4348	1.0658	0.9518	1.1190
12. Rumania	1.1977	0.8671	0.6080	0.5795	0.8131
13. Bulgaria	0.4557	0.5103	0.5357	0.5000	0.5004
14. LDC and its components	0.4045	0.4137	0.3703	0.4050	0.3984
15. UAR	0.3352	0.5817	0.4039	0.5441	0.4662
16. China	0.4067	0.4028	0.3453	0.3596	0.3786
17. India	0.3432	0.3552	0.3695	0.4204	0.3721

Although the Vanek third factor explanation is no longer deemed a correct solution to the Leontief Paradox, the possibility that natural resources might constitute a decisive factor in another context should not be ruled out. Table 5-1 shows the effect of deleting the influence of the following six natural resource vectors on the structure of bilateral Soviet Leontief Statistics: ferrous ores (1), nonferrous ores (3), coal (8), crude petroluem (9), natural gas (11), and unprocessed timber (51a),[5] by subtracting the direct-plus-indirect capital and labor contribution associated with the import replacements and exports of these sectors. If we begin by considering row 1 representing Soviet Leontief Statistics generated in U.S.S.R.-WORLD trade and compare them to their 66 sector counterparts in Table 4-1 we immediately discover that with the exception of 1955 the deletion of the influence of the natural resource sectors results in a decreased capital intensive export bias. This means that in the Soviet context, natural resources, as relatively capital intensive net export commodities, are responsible for a significant portion of the overall capital intensive export bias characteristic of U.S.S.R.-WORLD exchange. For the years 1955-1968 we find that the omission of natural resources reduces the capital intensive export bias an average amount of 45 percent from -1.52 to -0.83 bias units. However, in no individual year does the deletion of natural resources cause a capital intensive import bias to be transformed into a capital intensive export bias, which means that natural resources alone do not account for the fundamental capital intensive export bias noted in our previous analysis.

The potential significance of natural resources as a third factor, however, does not repose solely in the possibility of reversing our neoclassical factor proportions findings. Figure 5-1, illustrating the time trend of U.S.S.R.-WORLD Soviet Leontief Statistics based on 60 and 66 sector computations, affords us two extremely useful insights. First, we discover that the magnitude of the capital intensive export bias is a monotonically increasing function of time with or without the inclusion of the natural resource sectors. This is a very important finding. All students of socialist international trade know that the Soviet Union has reluctantly become the chief natural resource supplier in the Soviet Bloc.[6] Since the U.S.S.R. has become increasingly specialized in the net export of natural resources 1955-1968, one could have easily conjectured that the secular trend towards diminishing values of the U.S.S.R.-WORLD Soviet Leontief Statistic was caused entirely by changes in net natural resource flows. The deletion of the natural resource vectors proves that such a surmise is incorrect. The secular tendency towards an increasingly capital intensive export bias persists independently of the natural resources effect. Secondly, Figure 5-1 brings out the fact that the rate of increase of the capital intensive export bias is substantially greater when natural resources are included in the computation of Soviet factor proportions. The capital intensive export bias of the full 66 sector U.S.S.R.-WORLD Leontief Statistic increases 4.29 bias units, while the increase with natural resources excluded 1955-1968 is only 1.30 bias units. This means

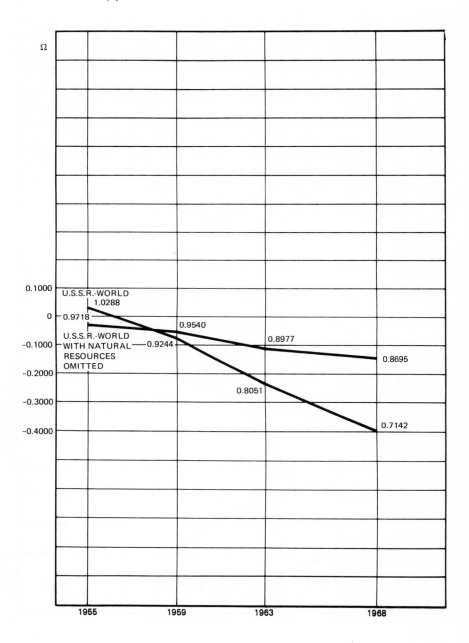

Figure 5-1. Comparison of Trends in Soviet Leontief Statistics With and Without the Influence of the Natural Resource Sectors Generated in U.S.S.R.-WORLD Trade Over the Period 1955-1968.

that the extraordinarily rapid decline in U.S.S.R.-WORLD Leontief Statistics discussed in Chapter 4 is in large part caused by the secular intensification of Soviet net natural resource exports. Moreover, the reduced rate of increase in the capital intensive export bias, resulting from the deletion of the influence of natural resources, is more compatible with trends in relative capital formation between the Soviet Union, the socialist and nonsocialist countries.[7] Thus, it seems that if not the decline itself, the excessively rapid rate of secular decline in U.S.S.R.-WORLD Leontief Statistics can be explained by treating natural resources as a third factor of growing relative abundance, which like capital is exported in exchange for labor intensive goods. This congenial interpretation has the joint virtues of identifying natural resources as a Heckscher-Ohlin rationally behaved third factor and of reconciling the relative Soviet rates of capital formation with the secular increase in the capital intensive export bias.

This interpretation however is somewhat misleading. Figure 5-2 breaks down the Soviet Leontief Statistic structure into its component parts. Note in particular the secular time trend in U.S.S.R.-CMEA Leontief Statistics with and without the exclusion of the natural resource sectors. The Soviet Leontief Statistics computed on the full 66 sector basis move from a labor intensive export bias of 3.48 bias units to a capital intensive export bias of 4.35 bias units. Using the same measure the initial *labor intensive export bias* is 3.98 bias units with natural resources omitted, which over a thirteen year period switches to a *capital intensive export bias* of 2.12 bias units. The net change in the former case is 7.76 and in the latter 6.03 bias units, which means that the natural resources sectors are responsible for a 28 percent intensification in the secular movement of Soviet factor proportions. Since we have already seen that in U.S.S.R.-WORLD trade natural resources cause a threefold increase in the capital intensive export bias, the effect of deleting the influence of natural resources in U.S.S.R.-CMEA exchange is relatively minor. This is a perplexing outcome in terms of the third factor hypothesis because the sharply increased level of Soviet specialization in natural resource exports occurs primarily in exchange with the Soviet Bloc. Logically, we would anticipate that the effect of natural resources as a third factor would make itself most strongly felt in U.S.S.R.-CMEA trade, yet Figure 5-2 reveals that the trend in Soviet factor proportion 1955-1968 is fundamentally similar with or without the inclusion of natural resources. This means that natural resources cannot be considered an especially important third factor in its most important domain, U.S.S.R.-CMEA trade, so that the excessive capital intensity of the Soviet export bias generated in trade with the CMEA noted in Chapter 4, section F, can be explained neither by differentials in factor availabilities,[8] nor by natural resources conceived of as a third factor. Thus the ostensible plausibility of the natural resource third factor hypothesis turns out to be illusory in the U.S.S.R.-CMEA case.

If we next consider whether Soviet bilateral factor proportions generated in trade with the less developed countries supports the third factor hypothesis, the

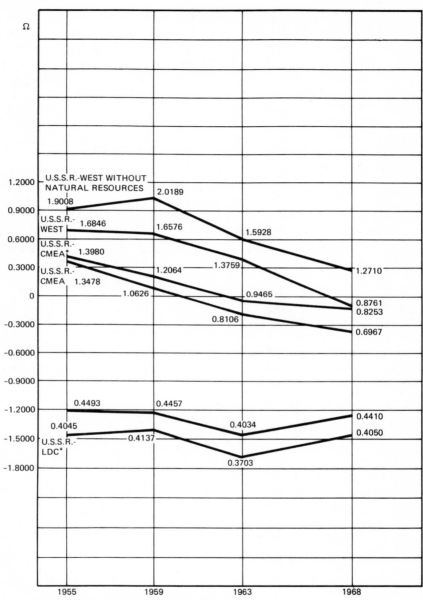

*Signifies that natural resources have been deleted

Figure 5-2. Comparison of Trends in Soviet Leontief Statistics Generated in U.S.S.R.-REGIONAL Trade With and Without the Inclusion of the Natural Resource Sectors Over the Period 1955-1968.

evidence in favor of the proposition is even less substantial than for the U.S.S.R.-CMEA example. Figure 5-3 shows that removing the influence of natural resources from the Soviet Leontief Statistics computed for all 66 sectors causes an increase in the capital intensity of the export bias. This result, the reverse of the U.S.S.R.-CMEA and U.S.S.R.-WEST cases, reflects the fact that natural resources function as net imports, rather than net exports in U.S.S.R.-LDC exchange. The time trends of U.S.S.R.-LDC Leontief Statistic values however are virtually unaffected by the removal of the influence of natural resources, which means that the time pattern of U.S.S.R.-LDC factor proportions cannot be explained by natural resources construed as a third independent factor.

Figure 5-2 also shows, however, that natural resources do tend to have some special influence in U.S.S.R.-WEST trade, where the deletion of the natural resource vectors modifies the rate and pattern of the Soviet Leontief Statistic time trend. Natural resources have a particularly strong effect on U.S.S.R.-WEST exchange in the 1955-1959 and 1963-1968 intervals, which a glance at Figure 5-2 will show was translated into an accelerated rate of decrease in the labor intensity of the U.S.S.R.-WEST export bias. Therefore it may be possible in part to describe the operation of the Soviet factor proportions mechanism in U.S.S.R.-WEST trade as a process where natural resource intensive commodities are exported in exchange for capital intensive imports; Soviet natural resources being relatively more abundant than Soviet labor. Whether or not this is a correct statement of true relative factor availabilities, it is clear that reliance on only two neoclassical aggregate factors masks a potentially important dimension of U.S.S.R.-WEST exchange by failing to show that capital intensive Western commodities are being imported not simply in exchange for labor intensive Soviet goods, but for a combination of labor and natural resource intensive items. This realization however does not mean that U.S.S.R.-WEST exchange is inconsistent with the principles of Heckscher-Ohlin theorem I. It implies only that the two factor neoclassical input aggregation is too restrictive to bring out all the salient aspects of the factor proportions situation in the single case of U.S.S.R.-WEST trade.

It remains to be demonstrated, however, that the deletion of the influence of natural resources does in fact result in a distribution of observations that conforms with Heckscher-Ohlin theorem I laws when our concern is for the relationship between Soviet Leontief Statistics and our per capita GNP proxy for capital labor availabilities. Figure 5-3, plotting the Soviet Leontief Statistic against per capita GNP, shows that the distribution of observations allowing for the deletion of natural resources remains fundamentally consistent with Heckscher-Ohlin theorem I. Only the U.S.S.R.-Polish observation falls outside of quadrants I and III. In addition, we find that a modest labor intensive bias is revealed by the regression line lying to the northwest of the U.S.S.R.-U.S.S.R. point. But Figure 5-4 reveals the importance of this labor intensive export bias,

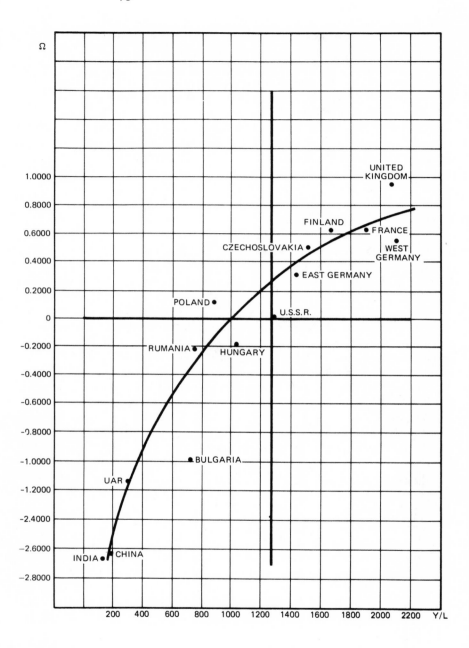

Figure 5-3. 1955-1968 Average Soviet Leontief Statistics With the Natural Resource Sectors Deleted, Generated in Trade With 13 Countries, Plotted as a Function of Average 1955-1968 Per Capita GNP.

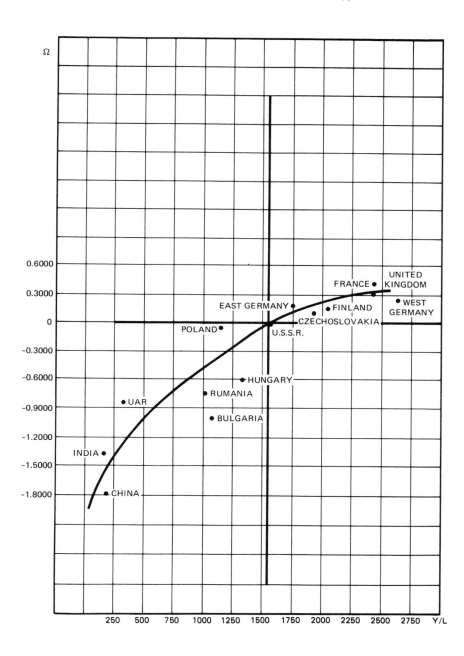

Figure 5-4. 1968 Soviet Leontief Statistics With Natural Resources Deleted, Generated in Trade With 13 Countries, Plotted Against 1968 GNP.

not present when natural resources are included in the computation of Soviet Leontief Statistics, is offset by the fact that the excessive secular trend towards an increasingly capital intensive export bias noted at the full 66 sector aggregation in 1968 disappears when the influence of natural resources is eliminated. Furthermore we find that a semi-logarithmic regression run on the average 1955-1968 60 sector aggregate yields an R of 0.9620, with a β coefficient equal to 2.25411, significant at the 0.995 confidence level, which explains 92.5 percent of the variation in the dependent variable.[9] Since this is precisely the result obtained when natural resources were included, it reconfirms the existence of the strong, fundamental consistency between the distribution of Soviet Leontief Statistics and the Heckscher-Ohlin theorem first observed in Chapter 4.

Thus, in sum, our investigation of the natural resources, third factor hypothesis in the Soviet context demonstrates that natural resources have significant independent explanatory power only in bilateral U.S.S.R.-WEST commodity exchange, and that on balance natural resources alter little the conclusions reached with the neoclassical aggregate factor alone. Since the third factor hypothesis is given only tenuous support, it would seem that the theoretically correct way of interpretating the structure of Soviet factor proportion is with the neoclassical factors used in Chapter 4, section F.

B. Soviet Leontief Statistics with Skilled Labor Treated as the Scarce Domestic Factor

The persistence of the Leontief Paradox in U.S.-WORLD trade over a fairly extended time period has prodded specialists in the field of international trade to formulate alternative theories to explain the existing pattern of American factor proportions. Some of the hypotheses put forward have been variants of the basic Heckscher-Ohlin theme, others like the product cycle hypothesis have struck out in entirely new directions.[10] Two especially important conjectures within the scope of the Heckscher-Ohlin tradition have stressed the significance of third factors, one emphasizing the notion of skilled labor as a strategic input, the other technology.[11] While conceptually distinct these factors turn out to be highly intercorrelated because skilled labor is a key input into high technology industries, and therefore it is convenient to test both hypotheses by the simple expedient of using a skilled labor variable as a proxy for both factors. The explicit introduction of the skilled labor variable opens up the possibility of viewing Soviet factor proportions afresh. Although our prior analysis has not produced any evidence for a Soviet equivalent of the American Leontief Paradox, skilled labor and technology could potentially play a very significant role in the Soviet economy so that a formal quantification of the impact of these variables is a matter of considerable interest even in the Soviet context where neoclassical variables accord well with the principles of Heckscher-Ohlin theorem I.

For input-output purposes the Russians define two categories of non-blue-collar skilled labor. The first category is defined as administrative-managerial supervisory and engineering personnel with completed higher education. The second category refers to the same group of job functions performed by workers who have not completed some form of higher educational program. Operating on the hypothesis that skilled labor-cum-technology is the truly scarce factor in the Soviet economy, in contrast to the neoclassical factor aggregate general labor, I constructed two new factor proportions ratios: S1/L and S2/L, where S1 refers to the first skilled labor category, S2 to the second and L to general labor. Soviet Leontief Statistics computed for these factor proportions ratios are presented in Tables 5-2 and 5-3. Looking at row 1 of each table we see that U.S.S.R.-WORLD trade is characterized by a modest skilled-labor intensive

Table 5-2

Soviet Leontief Statistics Computed for the Factor Proportion Ratio of Skilled Labor With Completed Higher Education to General Labor, Generated in Trade With 13 Countries for the Years 1955, 1959, 1963, 1968

Soviet Trade Pattern With	Soviet Leontief Statistics (S1/L) Year				
	1955	1959	1963	1968	1955-1968
1. WORLD	1.1034	1.0733	1.0649	0.9937	1.0588
2. WEST and its components	2.6503	2.8822	2.6612	2.0029	2.5492
3. United Kingdom	2.9577	3.3225	3.4966	2.1418	2.9800
4. West Germany	2.7284	2.2209	1.9865	2.0116	2.2369
5. France	1.7035	2.2835	2.3900	2.1326	2.1274
6. Finland	2.7526	3.1490	2.6219	1.6813	2.5512
7. CMEA and its components	1.6483	1.5275	1.1650	0.9838	1.3312
8. Czechoslovakia	2.7120	1.7666	1.6127	1.4103	1.8759
9. East Germany	2.8328	2.4139	1.7639	1.6613	2.1680
10. Hungary	1.2392	1.1582	0.9311	0.8217	1.0376
11. Poland	0.9391	1.5730	1.2400	1.1371	1.2223
12. Rumania	0.8690	0.7182	0.5311	0.5594	0.6694
13. Bulgaria	0.4617	0.5025	0.4805	0.4435	0.4721
14. LDC and its components	0.3191	0.3090	0.3285	0.3268	0.3208
15. UAR	0.6294	0.5422	0.2943	0.4104	0.4691
16. China	0.3156	0.2918	0.4392	0.3042	0.3377
17. India	0.3101	0.2661	0.2332	0.2613	0.2683

Table 5-3

Soviet Leontief Statistics Computed for the Factor Proportions Ratio of Skilled Labor Without Completed Higher Education to General Labor, Generated in Trade With 13 Countries in the Years 1955, 1959, 1963, 1968

Soviet Trade Pattern With	Soviet Leontief Statistics (S2/L) Year				
	1955	1959	1963	1968	1955-1968
1. WORLD	1.0658	1.0218	0.9986	0.9684	1.0137
2. WEST and its components	1.7629	1.8452	1.7636	1.4466	1.7046
3. United Kingdom	1.7569	1.8787	1.9261	1.4219	1.7460
4. West Germany	1.7928	1.6232	1.5036	1.5241	1.6109
5. France	1.2346	1.5185	1.4853	1.4324	1.4181
6. Finland	1.9466	2.0625	1.8118	1.2986	1.7799
7. CMEA and its components	1.4902	1.3320	1.0974	0.9797	1.2248
8. Czechoslovakia	1.9362	1.4338	1.3662	1.2330	1.4923
9. East Germany	2.0818	1.7523	1.3743	1.3567	1.6413
10. Hungary	1.1422	1.0535	0.8836	0.8216	0.9752
11. Poland	1.1664	1.5074	1.2235	1.1293	1.2567
12. Rumania	1.1152	0.9372	0.7278	0.7190	0.8748
13. Bulgaria	0.6134	0.6752	0.6425	0.5939	0.6313
14. LDC and its components	0.4642	0.4415	0.4332	0.4604	0.4498
15. UAR	0.5758	0.4978	0.3595	0.5132	0.4866
16. China	0.4630	0.4276	0.5076	0.3995	0.4494
17. India	0.5381	0.4411	0.4026	0.4176	0.4499

import bias, although in 1963 and 1968 a slight skilled labor intensive export bias develops. In addition, a very moderate secular tendency towards a decreased skilled labor import bias is discernible. On a regional basis we discover that the Soviet Union manifests a skilled labor import bias in its trade with the WEST and the CMEA, and a strong skilled labor intensive export bias in U.S.S.R.-LDC exchange. In terms of secular trends only U.S.S.R.-CMEA trade reveals a decisive tendency towards the diminution of its skilled labor intensive import bias.

Viewed from a third factor perspective the Soviet Leontief Statistics in Tables 5-2 and 5-3 suggest that the skilled labor-technology factor has not tended to promote a radical transformation in the commodity structure of Soviet international trade. Indeed, in regard to skilled labor-technology, the pattern of U.S.S.R.-WEST and U.S.S.R.-LDC factor proportions exhibits no decisive trend, suggesting that relative supplies of skilled labor, or the technology gap has not been altered in any fundamental way 1955-1968 vis-à-vis the WEST and the less developed countries.[12] This implies that the structure of Soviet commodity trade should have remained basically unchanged because the underlying factor proportions determining commodity flows, particularly in U.S.S.R.-WEST and U.S.S.R.-LDC trade have been relatively constant. Our study of capital, labor and natural resources factor proportions reveals however that the commodity structure of Soviet international trade has changed considerably, especially in U.S.S.R.-WEST trade, suggesting that as a third factor the skilled labor-technology variable has played a passive role, functioning more as a dependent rather than as an independent variable in relation to changes in Soviet commodity structure, and that the neo-classical aggregate factors conform better to Heckscher-Ohlin theorem I principles.[13] A decisive test of this interpretation requires that we obtain data on skilled labor stocks and the growth of these stocks over time in all thirteen countries employed in this study. Problems of skill definition, however, make a successful test of the Heckscher-Ohlin consistency of the skilled labor variable very remote. Therefore for the purpose of crude comparison I again use the per capita GNP proxy understood now as a measure of skilled labor and general labor availabilities. I assume that the capital-labor and skilled labor-labor availability distributions are in fact different, but that a positive association by level of development persists in both cases nonetheless. Since the per capita GNP proxy is not likely to be a very good instrumental variable we will dispense with regression analysis and only seek to verify whether there exists a tendency for Soviet Leontief Statistics measuring the skilled labor-general labor ratio to be consistent with Heckscher-Ohlin theorem I. Figures 5-5 and 5-6 reveal that most observations cluster in quadrants I and III, and suggest a semi-logarithmic plot, which implies that Soviet Leontief Statistics computed for skilled labor-general labor ratios are not inconsistent with the Heckscher-Ohlin approach. Given the questionable value of per capita GNP as our skilled labor-general labor instrumental variable, this is about all that we can credibly deduce. Thus, our discussion of the skilled labor-technology third factor must end on a somewhat inconclusive note. In sum, we find that U.S.S.R.-WORLD trade is characterized by a modest and slowly secularly declining skilled labor intensive import bias, that this skilled labor intensive import bias is particularly strong in U.S.S.R.-WEST exchange where the import bias has remained almost constant from 1955-1968, and that the structure of skilled labor-labor Soviet Leontief Statistics is in rough accord with Heckscher-Ohlin theorem I. However, when contrasted with the dynamic movement in the Soviet Leontief Statistics computed from neoclassical aggregate factors the skilled labor third factor seems more like a determined rather than a determining variable. The skilled labor-general labor Soviet Leontief Statistic from this perspective therefore tells us what the effect of changes in Soviet commodity structure have been on the embodiment of skilled labor-technology in Soviet traded goods, but not how skilled labor determined Soviet commodity structure.

On balance our analysis of the third factor hypothesis has shown that the

84

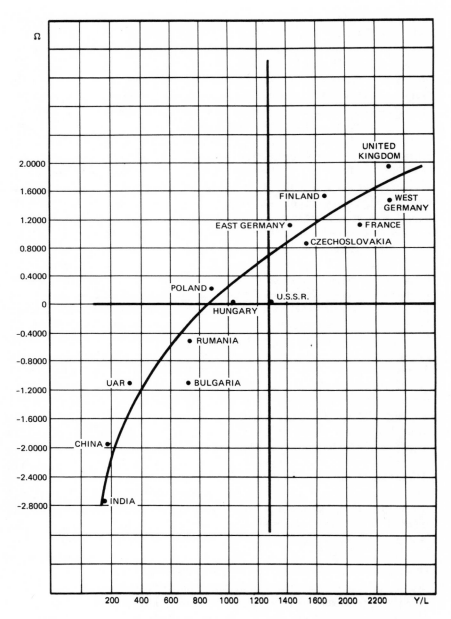

Figure 5-5. Soviet Leontief Statistics for the Skilled Labor-General Labor Ratio (S1/L), Generated in Soviet Trade With 13 Countries, Plotted Against Per Capita GNP, Average Values for the Period 1955-1968.

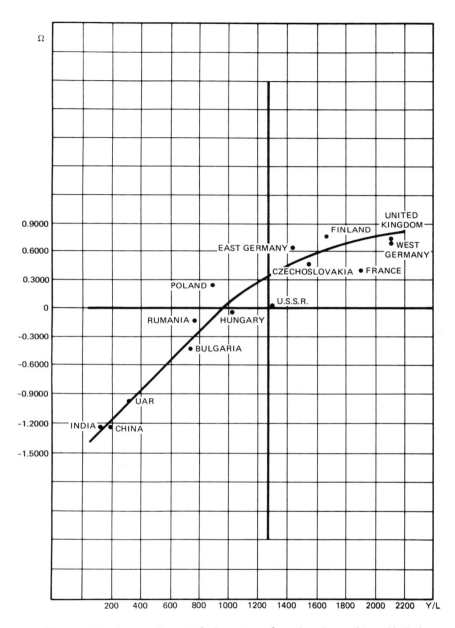

Figure 5-6. Soviet Leontief Statistics for the Secondary Skilled-Labor-General Labor Ratio (S2/L), Generated in Soviet Trade With 13 Countries, Plotted Against Per Capita GNP, Average Values for the Period 1955-1968.

neoclassical factor aggregates, capital and labor adequately describe the fundamental transformations in the commodity structure of Soviet international trade. However, we find that U.S.S.R.-WEST trade cannot be satisfactorily understood without appreciating the role played by natural resources as a third factor, or the extraordinary passive character of the skilled labor-technology variable in the Soviet context.

6

A Comparison of U.S. and U.S.S.R. Factor Proportions and Their Consistency with the Principles of Heckscher-Ohlin Theorem I

During the course of our analysis of Soviet Leontief Statistics we have had occasion to compare American and Soviet factor proportions in a somewhat haphazard manner. In this section we shall make these comparisons more systematic in order to evaluate the Soviet findings in a broader context. We shall explicitly investigate the manner in which American Leontief Statistics conform to the principles of Heckscher-Ohlin theorem I, using neoclassical factors, natural resources as a third factor, and the skilled labor-general labor variable. In Appendix B we also consider the Heckscher-Ohlin rationality of American Leontief Statistics utilizing Baldwin's procedure of correlating net exports by industry with the ratio of direct-plus-indirect factor requirements needed to sustain a dollar's worth of output in that industry.

A. The Rationale for Comparing American and Soviet Factor Proportions

From a theoretical point of view the commodity structure of American and Soviet international trade is influenced by a very significant common factor; the great territorial expanse of both countries makes each a "natural market area," self-sufficient and internally oriented. Few other economies possess this characteristic, which is important because it implies that the composition of commodity trade will not be dominated by special locational or natural resource factors. In addition to this "natural market area" argument there are also practical considerations pressing in favor of a comparison of American and Soviet Leontief Statistics. First, American factor proportions have been studied extensively by a variety of scholars, which means that the statistical reliability of the U.S. results is well established. Second, an American input-output table is available for the year 1958. Since the Soviet table was constructed for the Russian economy of 1959, the temporal aspect of a Soviet-American comparison poses no difficulty. Third, in addition to the temporal factor, the structure of the interindustry flows matrices are conformible, the U.S. table containing 82 vectors, compared with the original Soviet table composed of 83 sectors. This comparability in aggregation levels means that the Leontief Statistics generated by the commodity trade of each country will not be influenced by informational factors stemming from the use of substantially different degrees of sectoral aggregation. Fourth, the capital and labor vectors are similarly defined in both tables, ensuring against distortion arising from incompatibly defined factor inputs.

B. American Factor Proportions

The latest and, in many respects, most comprehensive study of American factor proportions is Robert Baldwin's article "Determinants of the Commodity Structure of U.S. Trade," which appeared in the March 1971 issue of the *AER*. All the data used in our comparison of American and Soviet Leontief Statistics comes from this source. Although Baldwin analyzes the determinants of American commodity structure from many angles, he does not, unfortunately, study the bilateral pattern of U.S. factor proportions on the same comprehensive scale undertaken in our work on Soviet factor proportions. In contrast to the Soviet case, where bilateral exchange between thirteen countries and three regions is assessed over a thirteen year period, Baldwin limits his bilateral analysis to two countries and three geographical regions in 1962; Canada and Japan; O.E.C.D. Europe, the Less Developed Countries and OTHER. The first three territorial units are self-explanatory, but the Less Developed Countries and OTHER designations require comment. The Less Developed Countries aggregate is defined by Baldwin as, Africa, Asia, other than China and Japan, and the Western Hemisphere, other than Canada and the U.S. Although this definition does not conflict with our use of the term less developed countries, in a practical sense the Soviet and American LDC concepts are quite distinct because the United States and the U.S.S.R. trade bilaterally with different subsets, and in different proportions, with the same subsets of the developing nations. Therefore, in appraising our subsequent findings the reader should bear in mind that the Less Developed Countries designation refers to different entities in the American and Soviet contexts. To make this point clear we shall in the future refer to the less developed trading partners of the United States as LDC*, in contrast to the notation LDC used for those developing nations trading with the Soviet Union.

Baldwin's aggregate category OTHER refers to two strikingly different subgroups, Oceania and the CMEA. Of the two, Oceania accounts for 80 percent and the CMEA for 19 percent of American bilateral exchange with the OTHER group. The unfortunate juxtaposition of these dissimilar subgroups makes interpretation of American bilateral factor proportions with the OTHER category a particularly ambiguous exercise. Nonetheless, since Baldwin's bilateral study represents the most up to date and comprehensive work available, we therefore use his categories with the appropriate cautions.

C. American Factor Proportions Computed with
Neoclassical Factor Inputs, Capital and Labor

American Leontief Statistics for 1962 computed by Baldwin are presented in Table 6-1 along with their Soviet counterparts where available for 1963. Row 1

Table 6-1

American Leontief Statistics Generated in U.S. Trade With Five Areas in 1962, Contrasted Where Applicable With Soviet Leontief Statistics Generated in U.S.S.R. Trade With Similar Regions

U.S. Trade Pattern With	U.S.S.R. Trade Pattern With	American Leontief[a] Statistics 1962	Soviet Leontief Statistics 1963
1. World	World	1.27	0.8051
2. Canada		1.41	–
3. Oceania-CMEA	CMEA	1.42	0.8106
4. O.E.C.D.: Europe	WEST	0.87	1.3759
5. Japan		0.73	–
6. LDC*	LDC	1.78	0.4034

[a]American Leontief Statistics are taken from Baldwin, "Determinants of the Commodity Structure of U.S. Trade," AER, March 1971, Table 1, p. 134, and Table 4, p. 140.

reveals, as we have already mentioned, that U.S.-WORLD factor proportions demonstrate a capital intensive import bias, in sharp contrast to the capital intensive export bias characteristic of U.S.S.R.-WORLD exchange. On a continuous and symmetrically defined factor proportions scale American factor proportions show a capital intensive *import bias* of 2.7 bias units in contrast to a 2.4 bias unit capital intensive *export bias* for the Soviet Union, which reveals that although American and Soviet biases are of opposite sign, they reflect similar magnitudes. Rows 3, 4, and 6 demonstrate that not only are American and Soviet biases of opposite sign in trade with the WORLD as a whole, but the direction of the factor proportions bias diverges for all bilateral subgroups as well. The bias unit magnitudes however are not, as in the U.S.S.R.-WORLD and the U.S.-WORLD cases, proportional. In itself, the fact that the United States and U.S.S.R. exhibit biases of opposite sign in bilateral trade with various subgroups, means little. To really perceive the meaning of the American factor proportions structure we must apply the Heckscher-Ohlin theorem I test used on our Soviet data in Chapters 4 and 5. Figure 6.1 presents a scatter of American Leontief Statistic observations plotted against a per capita GNP proxy for capital-labor availabilities. The per capita GNP figures were computed in strict conformity with the methodology applied in our study of Soviet factor proportions. The details of the computation are provided in Appendix D. To test the Heckscher-Ohlin validity of the American Leontief Statistics a set of coordinate axes has been drawn with the hypothetical U.S.-U.S. observation as the origin, dividing the graph into four quadrants. As before, conformity to Heckscher-Ohlin theorem I principles requires that in its bilateral exchange with countries relatively better endowed with capital, the United States should import capital intensive goods, and where less relatively well endowed with capital, the United States should export capital intensive goods. Since no one doubts that the United States is relatively better endowed with capital than all other countries, a fact reflected well by the per capita proxy, all Leontief

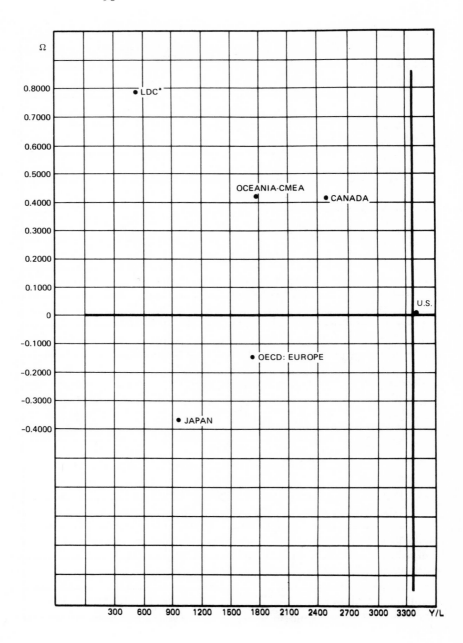

Figure 6-1. American Leontief Statistics Generated in Bilateral Trade With Five Regions in 1962, Plotted Against 1962 Per Capita GNP.

Statistic observations obeying the laws of Heckscher-Ohlin theorem I should fall in quadrant III. Moreover, if in addition to possessing the appropriate Heckscher-Ohlin characteristics, the multi-national production functions linking factor availabilities with our per capita GNP variable display Cobb-Douglas properties, we would also expect to see some tendency for a semi-logarithmic clustering of points with the regression line passing through the factor proportions neutral U.S.-U.S. point. Figure 6-1 shows that there exists no perceptible tendency for U.S. factor proportions to conform with the principles of Heckscher-Ohlin theorem I. Of the five independent observations, three fall into quadrant two, which means that they are negatively correlated with Heckscher-Ohlin processes. Worse still the extreme U.S.S.R.-LDC* case, which if the Heckscher-Ohlin mechanism were operative should exhibit a strong capital intensive export bias, in fact demonstrates the opposite property, a strong capital intensive import bias.[1] These results contrast in a startling way with the excellent Heckscher-Ohlin theorem I consistent behavior of the analogous Soviet case shown in Figure 4-7, where all observations fall in the appropriate quadrants and form a semi-logarithmic cluster passing through the factor proportions neutral U.S.S.R.-U.S.S.R. point. In the light of these findings it is no wonder that Western analysts have sought third factor explanations of the determinants of the U.S. commodity structure.

D. Natural Resources as a Third Factor Explanation of the U.S. Commodity Structure

Impelled by the Heckscher-Ohlin inconsistency of American factor proportions Baldwin tested a variety of frequently voiced alternative explanations of the determinants of the U.S. trade pattern. Because of its prominent place in the literature, special attention was focused on the third factor, natural resources hypothesis. Table 6-2 bears on this issue, presenting American Leontief Statistics which exclude the influence of the natural resource sectors,[2] and supplies analogous Soviet Leontief Statistic values where applicable. Row 1 reveals that the deletion of the natural resource vectors in both Soviet and American cases shifts the Leontief Statistics in the direction of factor proportions neutrality, the U.S. figure showing a capital intensive import bias of only 0.40 bias units, while the Soviet value displays a capital intensive export bias reduced from 2.42 to 1.11 bias units. Note also in this regard that by itself the deletion of the influence of agriculture imparts an additional capital intensive import bias of 1.4 bias units to the U.S.-WORLD Leontief Statistic.[3] Since agriculture is lumped together with natural resources according to Baldwin's definition,[4] we can ascertain the pure natural resources effect by subtracting 1.4 bias units from the figure in row 1, column 3, which reveals that both the United States and the U.S.S.R. manifest *exactly the same capital intensive export bias*, 1.11 bias units,

Table 6-2

American Leontief Statistics Excluding Natural Resources, Generated in Trade With Five Areas in 1962, Compared With Analogous Soviet Leontief Statistics Where Applicable

U.S. Trade Pattern With	U.S.S.R. Trade Pattern With	American Leontief Statistics for 1962	Soviet Leontief Statistics for 1963
1. World	WORLD	1.04	0.8977
2. Canada		1.15	–
3. Oceania-CMEA	CMEA	1.33	0.9465
4. O.E.C.D.: Europe	WEST	0.93	1.5928
5. Japan		0.84	–
6. LDC*	LDC	1.14	0.3703

in their trade with the world as a whole. No normative value can be placed on this finding, especially given the fact that Baldwin's definition of natural resources includes natural resource processing industries excluded from the natural resource category in the computation of the Soviet Leontief Statistic. Nevertheless, it is interesting that the deletion of the natural resource vectors reveals a merging of the factor proportions structure of these two countries.

Unfortunately, Baldwin does not supply us with bilateral American Leontief Statistics which exclude the influence of agriculture, so that we are unable to estimate the effect of deleting natural resources per se from American commodity trade with Canada, OECD: Europe, Oceania-CMEA, Japan and LDC*. Considering the figures presented in Table 6-2 as they stand, including as they do both agriculture and natural resource processing industries, we discover an important unifying characteristic. The removal of natural resources in every case diminishes the bias exhibited in the unadjusted Leontief Statistic measure, whether that bias initially appears in exports or imports. The Soviet case does not demonstrate an analogous regularity.

The overall result of this across the boards diminution of American bilateral factor proportions bias is shown in Figure 6-2. The Japanese and the O.E.C.D.: European observations exhibit a decreased capital intensive export bias, while the Canadian, Oceania-CMEA, and LDC* observations manifest the opposite tendency. The most significant movement occurs in American-LDC* exchange which shows a decline in the capital intensive import bias of 6.4 bias units. However, as important as these changes are, they still do not make the American case consistent with the principles of Heckscher-Ohlin theorem I. Despite the third factor effect of natural resources, three of the five observations continue to fall in quadrant II, implying a negative correlation between the structure of American bilateral factor proportions and Heckscher-Ohlin causality. These results again contrast sharply with our analysis of the third factor impact of

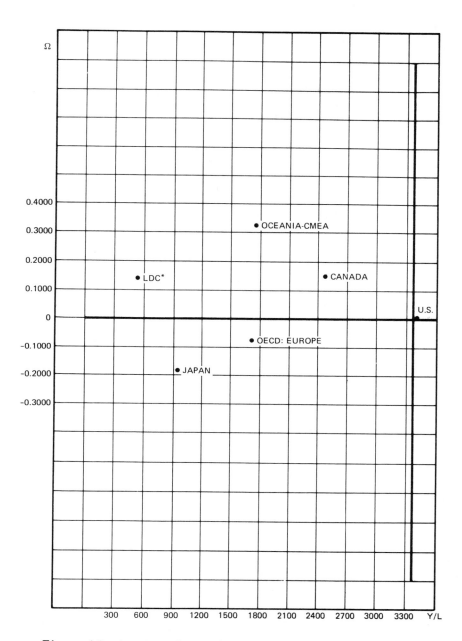

Figure 6-2. American Leontief Statistics With Natural Resources Deleted, Generated in Trade Between the U.S. and Five Other Countries in 1962, Plotted Against 1962 Per Capita GNP.

natural resources on Soviet Leontief Statistics. Figure 5-3 demonstrates that the deletion of the natural resource sectors yield a set of observations consistent with Heckscher-Ohlin theorem I, exhibiting a semi-logarithmic cluster of observations, passing through the U.S.S.R.-U.S.S.R. factor proportions neutrality point. This result not only yielded an R^2 value fully as good as the neoclassical factor case but was found to have special explanatory power for U.S.-WEST exchange and to partially explain the secular tendency towards a capital intensive export bias found when neoclassical factors were used.

In sum, comparing U.S. and U.S.S.R. third natural resource factor explanations we discover that despite the general decrease in the magnitude of American factor proportions bias resulting from the removal of natural resource influence, American Leontief Statistic observations continue to be inconsistent with Heckscher-Ohlin principles, in direct contrast to the Soviet case, which exhibits strong Heckscher-Ohlin consistency.

E. Skilled Labor and Technology as an Alternative Third Factor Explanation of the U.S. Commodity Structure

Within the compass of the Heckscher-Ohlin model there exists one additional third factor explanation that commands broad support among international trade theorists. I refer here to the skilled labor-technology variable which receives explicit endorsement from Baldwin as the most promising explanation of American factor proportions.[5] Table 6-3 presents American and Soviet Leontief Statistics computed for skilled labor-general labor factor proportions ratios. As Table 6-2 shows, Baldwin employs two distinct definitions for skilled American labor. The first ($\hat{S}1$) includes professional, technical, and managerial personnel, regardless of educational background, a group that comprises approximately 12 percent of the American labor force. His second ($\hat{S}2$) definition includes engineers and scientists alone, again without educational distinction. This group constitutes 1.8 percent of the American work force. Unfortunately, comparable Soviet skill definitions also presented in Table 6-3 diverge in important respects. Skilled labor of the first grade, administrative-managerial, supervisory, and engineering personnel, unlike their American analogue, are defined to include only individuals who have completed higher educations, which restricts the share of this category to 1.2 percent of the Soviet labor force. On the other hand, the second Soviet skill group defined without regard to educational level and constituting 4.4 percent of the Soviet work force is comprised of the same skills as category 1, but is not restricted to scientists and engineers as in the American case.[6] Therefore it must be recognized that since American and Soviet skill definitions are to some degree inconsistent, the possibility arises that differences in observed skilled labor-general labor factor proportions are attributable to definitional distinctions.

A glance at Table 6-3, column 3, reveals that the skilled labor-technology

Table 6-3

American Leontief Statistics Computed for Skilled Labor to General Labor Factor Proportions Generated in U.S. Bilateral Trade With Five Areas in 1962, Contrasted With Analogous Soviet Leontief Statistics for 1963 Where Available

U.S. Trade Pattern With	U.S.S.R. Trade Pattern With	American Leontief[e] Statistics 1962		Soviet Leontief[f] Statistics 1963	
		$\hat{S}1/L^a$	$\hat{S}2/L^b$	$S1/L^c$	$S2/L^d$
1. WORLD	WORLD	1.0549	0.8132	1.0649	0.9986
2. Canada		1.0787	0.9213	–	–
3. Oceania-CMEA	CMEA	0.6168	0.2710	1.1650	1.0974
4. O.E.C.D.: Europe	WEST	1.1579	1.0947	2.6612	1.7636
5. Japan		1.0286	0.8952	–	–
6. LDC*	LDC	1.1481	0.9259	0.3285	0.4332

[a]$\hat{S}1/L$ designates the fact that the American Leontief Statistics recorded in this column are defined as the ratio of professional, technical and managerial personnel with no educational distinction, to general labor.

[b]$\hat{S}2/L$ refers to the same concept except $\hat{S}2$ is defined as scientists and engineers only.

[c]$S1/L$ designates the fact that the Soviet Leontief Statistics recorded in this column are defined as the ratio of administrative-managerial, supervisory and engineering personnel with completed higher education.

[d]$S2/L$ refers to the same concept, except S2 has no educational restriction.

[e]American Leontief Statistics are taken from Baldwin, "Determinants of the Commodity Structure of U.S. Trade," AER, March 1971, Table 1, p. 134, Table 2, p. 136, and Table 4, p. 140.

[f]For Soviet Leontief Statistics see Tables 5-2 and 5-3.

variable defined as professional, technical, and managerial personnel fails to explain the Heckscher-Ohlin inconsistency of American factor proportions. Instead of demonstrating a skilled labor intensive export bias, predicted by the third skilled labor-technology factor hypothesis, the U.S.-WORLD Leontief Statistic exhibits a skilled labor intensive import bias. Moreover, if as in the Soviet case, we tentatively accept the per capita GNP proxy for demonstration purposes as a crudely acceptable proxy for underlying skilled labor-labor availabilities, Figure 6-3 shows that the skilled labor intensive import bias characterizes U.S. bilateral exchange as well, since four of the five bilateral Leontief Statistics fall in quadrant II, instead of appearing in quadrant III in accordance with the laws of Heckscher-Ohlin theorem I. Nevertheless, one conspicuous new development is the appearance of an intense skilled labor export bias in American trade with the heterogeneous geographical aggregate Oceania-CMEA, which suggests that the skilled labor technology variable plays a very special role in determining the commodity structure of U.S.-OTHER trade. However, in view of the problematic correlation between the true underlying skill availabilities and the per capita GNP variable, all the findings above should be regarded as tendencies rather than exact functional relationships.

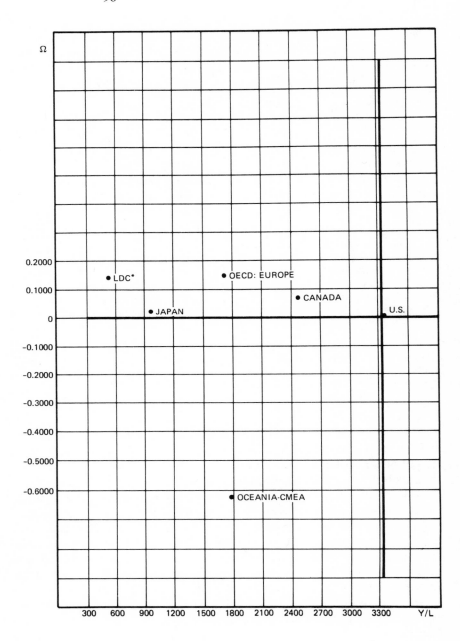

Figure 6-3. American Leontief Statistics Computed for the First Skilled Labor-General Labor Variable (S1/L), Generated in U.S. Trade With Five Areas in 1962, Plotted Against 1962 Per Capita GNP.

Subject to the same qualification, the second American measure of the skilled-labor technology variable places American factor proportions in a very different light. The American Leontief Statistics computed for the ratio of scientists and engineers to labor, presented in Table 6-3, column 4, and displayed graphically in Figure 6-4 is clearly consistent with Heckscher-Ohlin theorem I. The U.S.-WORLD Leontief Statistic exhibits a strong skilled labor intensive export bias of 2.30 bias units, while in bilateral exchange four of the five observations fall in quadrant III, in conformity with Heckscher-Ohlin causality. A comparison of Figures 6-3 and 6-4 establishes the fundamental similarity of the two scatters, which are differentiated from each other by a homogeneous downward shift in Figure 6-4 of the point scatter observed in Figure 6-3. This homogeneous shift away from a skilled labor intensive import bias towards a skilled labor export bias suggests that it is not skilled labor in general, but scientists and engineers in particular which constitute the relatively abundant third factor that determines the commodity structure of American trade. Moreover, since Baldwin specifically identifies scientists and engineers as a research and development proxy, it would probably be correct to surmise that it is technology per se rather than the labor skill of these engineers and scientists that determines the structure of American comparative advantage in commodity trade. Thus, Baldwin's judgment that skilled labor and technology are in large part responsible for the Leontief Paradox appears not to be misplaced. However, this point should not be exaggerated. Figure 6-4 shows that factor proportions based on the technology variable are consonant with Heckscher-Ohlin theorem I in only the most general way. No coherent relationship appears to link the observations in the second quadrant. While the per capita GNP measure is admittedly a weak proxy for relative achievement in technology, one would anticipate a stronger positive correlation between per capita GNP and American factor proportions. The enormously greater technology intensive export bias exhibited in U.S.-OTHER, in comparison with U.S.-LDC* is especially instructive in this regard. Furthermore, a comparison with the Soviet case depicted in Figures 5-5 and 5-6, which reveals a much stricter consistency with the principles of Heckscher-Ohlin theorem I, suggests that no simple, two or even three factor analysis adequately describes the complex forces determining the commodity structure of American trade.

In sum our analysis demonstrates that the commodity structure of American international trade can be reconciled in a modest way with Heckscher-Ohlin theorem I by discerning the third factor role played by technology in American bilateral exchange. However, the determinants of American comparative advantage appear to be so complex that the Heckscher-Ohlin theorem constitutes only a partial explanation for the U.S. trade pattern. On the other hand, viewed in the mirror of the American experience, the remarkable concordance between the structure of bilateral Soviet factor proportions and Heckscher-Ohlin laws, particularly in the neoclassical case, may be a reflection of the fact that in the

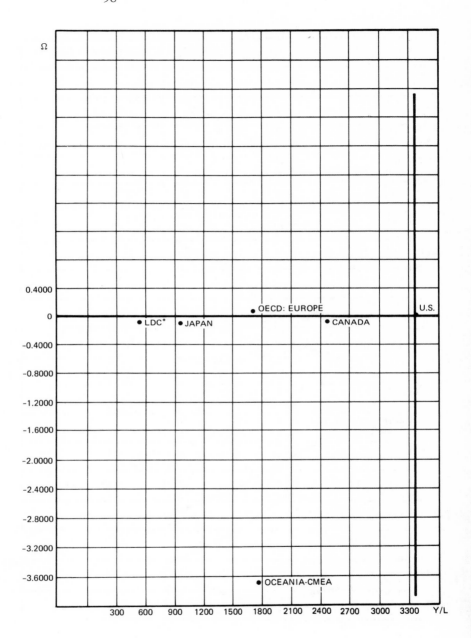

Figure 6-4. American Leontief Statistics Computed for the Second Skilled Labor-General Labor Variable (S2/L), Generated in Trade With Five Areas in 1962, Plotted Against 1962 Per Capita GNP.

relatively simpler Soviet economic environment, technology plays a less important role than in the American context, so that the Heckscher-Ohlin mechanism is left undisturbed by the interference of alternative influences.

Part III
Compositional Trends in Soviet Traded Goods and Soviet Factor Proportions

7

The Relationship Between Commodity Flow and Factor Proportion Trends in Soviet Bilateral Trade

Although our analysis of Soviet factor proportions has illuminated the Heckscher-Ohlin theorem I rationality of Soviet bilateral trade and has demonstrated that neither natural resources nor agricultural goods are responsible for the observed results,[1] it is nevertheless useful to ascertain whether there exist identifiable trends in the commodity structure of Soviet traded goods associated with trends in Soviet factor proportions. The justification for studying trends in Soviet commodity structure in the Heckscher-Ohlin context is twofold. First and most importantly a strong association between trends in commodity flows and factor proportions raises the possibility that political policy decisions regarding the structure of bilateral commodity exchange has fortuitously caused Soviet factor proportions to conform to a Heckscher-Ohlin theorem I rational pattern. Whether the causal relationship actually runs from commodity trends to factor proportions, or vice-versa as the Heckscher-Ohlin theory stipulates, cannot be unequivocally ascertained. The existence of an association between commodity trends and factor proportions cannot prove, but rather can only suggest the possibility that exogenous forces account for the ostensible Heckscher-Ohlin rationality of Soviet factor proportions. Second, assuming for the moment that trends in Soviet commodity structure are completely governed by opportunity costs, it is still interesting to establish how the Heckscher-Ohlin mechanism worked itself out concretely in the historical pattern of Soviet bilateral commodity exchange.

After much experimentation with alternative classification schemes it was found that four commodity categories best brought out the nature of aggregate bilateral commodity flows in the Soviet context: natural resources, heavy industrial, light industrial, and agricultural goods. The strong correlation between trends in the flows of these four commodity groups and trends in Soviet factor proportions can be readily demonstrated by recomputing Soviet Leontief Statistics using only natural resources, heavy industrial, light industrial, and agricultural categories instead of the full 66 commodity breakdown.[2] Table 7-1 presents factor proportion results obtained both from four and 66 sector classification. The correlation is remarkably good, indicating that direct-plus-indirect factor ratios do indeed aggregate into four distinct classes, and that Soviet factor proportions can profitably be analyzed in terms of these four commodity categories without a serious loss of information.[3] A regression specifying that Soviet Leontief Statistics computed on the four sector normalized basis are a linear function of normalized factor proportions calculated using

Table 7-1

A Comparison of Soviet Leontief Statistics Generated in Bilateral Exchange With the WORLD, and Its Components BLOCs, 1955-1968, Measured on a 66 and 4 Sector Basis

Soviet Trade Pattern With	Year	Soviet Leontief Statistics $\Omega 66$	$\Omega 4$
1. WORLD	1955	1.0288	0.9741
2. WORLD	1959	0.9244	0.8686
3. WORLD	1963	0.8051	0.7816
4. WORLD	1968	0.7142	0.7595
5. WEST	1955	1.6846	1.3154
6. WEST	1959	1.6576	1.3165
7. WEST	1963	1.3759	1.0291
8. WEST	1968	0.8761	0.7940
9. CMEA	1955	1.3478	1.3320
10. CMEA	1959	1.0626	1.0533
11. CMEA	1963	0.8106	0.8830
12. CMEA	1968	0.6967	0.8249
13. LDC	1955	0.4493	0.4767
14. LDC	1959	0.4457	0.4843
15. LDC	1963	0.4034	0.4299
16. LDC	1968	0.4410	0.5066

66 sectors yields an R^2 = 0.9671 with a β coefficient of 0.758, significant at the 0.995 confidence level.[4]

Having established that trends in the bilateral exchange of natural resources, heavy industrial, light industrial, and agricultural goods are highly correlated with trends in Soviet factor proportions let us proceed to identify their detailed pattern.

A. The Relationship Between Soviet Factor Proportions Generated in U.S.S.R.-WORLD Exchange and Transformations in the Commodity Composition of Soviet Traded Goods

Table 7-2 records the time trend in the commodity group composition of Soviet imports and exports, represented graphically in Figure 7-1. Taking imports first and concentrating on the lower panel we find that two groups, light and heavy industrial goods, increased their share in total Soviet imports while the natural resource and agricultural categories decreased reciprocally. Since light industrial

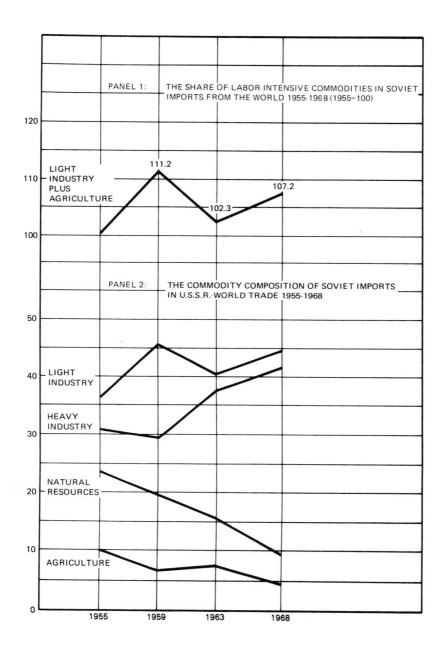

Figure 7-1. The Embodied Factor and Commodity Composition of Soviet Imports from the WORLD 1955-1968.

Table 7-2

The Commodity Composition of Soviet Traded Goods in U.S.S.R.-WORLD Exchange 1955-1968

I. Imports

Commodity Group	Commodity Group Shares of Soviet Imports from the WORLD in Percentages[a]			
	1955	1959	1963	1968
1. Natural Resources	23.2	19.4	15.4	9.0
2. Heavy Industry	30.8	29.4	37.4	41.6
3. Light Industry	36.1	45.1	40.0	44.6
4. Agriculture	10.0	6.2	7.2	4.8

II. Exports

Commodity Group	Commodity Group Shares of Soviet Exports from the WORLD in Percentages			
	1955	1959	1963	1968
1. Natural Resources	33.0	38.0	45.0	43.1
2. Heavy Industry	21.7	24.0	24.3	27.3
3. Light Industry	31.9	24.8	23.2	22.8
4. Agriculture	13.4	13.2	7.6	6.8

[a]Both imports and exports are valued at domestic wholesale prices net of turnover taxes levied on final consumption.

and agricultural goods are relatively labor intensive classifications and natural resources and heavy industrial goods relatively capital intensive activities, observed trends in the commodity composition of Soviet imports offset each other in regard to the average factor intensity of these imports. However, the upper panel, which represents an index of the share of the labor intensive commodity aggregates—light industry and agriculture—in Soviet imports from the WORLD, displays an erratic, but definitely upward trend in the average labor intensity of Soviet imports.

The commodity composition of Soviet exports demonstrates a very different pattern. It is the capital intensive commodity aggregates, natural resources and heavy industrial goods that increase their share in Soviet exports while the labor intensive groups progressively decline. The upper panel of Figure 7-2 shows that the combined effect of the trends in natural resources and heavy industry is a sharp and progressive rise in the share of capital intensive goods in Soviet exports. If we recall that the Leontief Statistic is a ratio of the import replacement capital-labor to the export capital-labor ratio, it is apparent that either a rise in the average labor intensity of import-replacement goods or a rise in the average capital intensity of exports will result in declining values for the Leontief Statistic itself. In U.S.S.R.-WORLD trade both these effects combined to produce a progressively increasing capital intensive export bias, or put

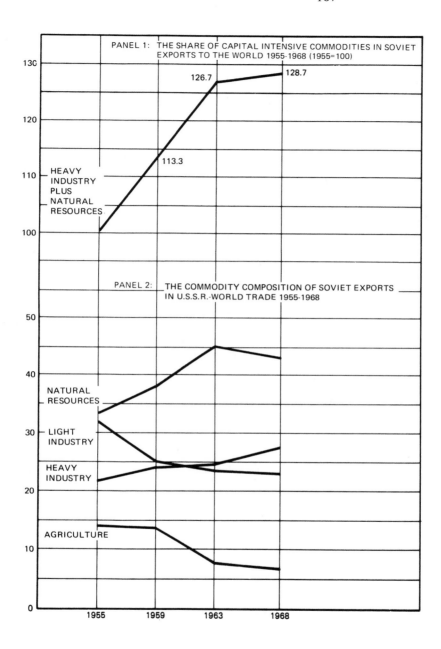

Figure 7-2. The Embodied Factor and Commodity Composition of Soviet Exports to the WORLD 1955-1968.

somewhat differently, trends in Soviet factor proportions studied in Chapters 4-6 are associated with changes in the commodity structure of Soviet traded goods reflecting a policy of planned increases in the share of consumers' goods in Soviet imports, paid for by planned increases in the share of producers' goods and natural resources in Soviet exports. Moreover, since it is well known that the Soviets have been upgrading the political importance of domestic consumption relative to investment in producers' goods, the observed change in the structure of Soviet traded goods is consistent with the announced objectives of the Soviet government, and thereby buttresses the possibility that factor proportion trends are the outcome of political considerations rather than Heckscher-Ohlin processes.

B. The Relationship Between Soviet Factor Proportions
Generated in U.S.S.R.-CMEA and U.S.S.R.-WEST Exchange
and Transformations in the Commodity Composition
of Soviet Traded Goods

With the aid of Tables 7-3 and 7-4, and their graphical counterparts in Figures 7-3–7-6, it can easily be shown that the same forces governing the changing composition of traded goods in U.S.S.R.–WORLD exchange are at work in U.S.S.R.–CMEA and U.S.S.R.-WEST trade. The upper panels of Figures 7-3 and

Table 7-3

The Commodity Composition of Soviet Traded Goods in U.S.S.R.-CMEA Exchange 1955-1968

I. Imports

Commodity Group	Commodity Group Shares of Soviet Imports from the CMEA in Percentages			
	1955	1959	1963	1968
1. Natural Resources	28.8	19.2	15.3	11.1
2. Heavy Industry	49.5	46.8	48.6	48.4
3. Light Industry	17.4	30.3	32.2	38.5
4. Agriculture	4.3	3.7	3.9	2.0

II. Exports

Commodity Group	Commodity Group Shares of Soviet Exports to the CMEA in Percentages			
	1955	1959	1963	1968
1. Natural Resources	29.2	40.3	46.6	42.8
2. Heavy Industry	19.7	16.0	21.2	28.6
3. Light Industry	34.8	28.3	22.0	20.8
4. Agriculture	16.2	15.4	10.2	7.8

Table 7-4

The Commodity Composition of Soviet Traded Goods in U.S.S.R.-WEST Exchange 1955-1968

I. Imports

Commodity Group	Commodity Group Shares of Soviet Imports from the WEST in Percentages			
	1955	1959	1963	1968
1. Natural Resources	26.2	32.5	19.0	10.4
2. Heavy Industry	54.6	47.3	61.0	58.6
3. Light Industry	19.2	20.0	19.7	30.4
4. Agriculture	0.	0.2	0.3	0.6

II. Exports

Commodity Group	Commodity Group Shares of Soviet Exports to the WEST in Percentages			
	1955	1959	1963	1968
1. Natural Resources	43.8	47.5	60.4	65.4
2. Heavy Industry	5.5	3.9	3.7	8.6
3. Light Industry	32.1	27.5	21.6	17.1
4. Agriculture	18.6	21.2	14.4	8.8

7-5 demonstrate that the consumers' goods share of Soviet imports from the CMEA and the WEST increase with time. In the U.S.S.R.-CMEA case the upward consumers' goods trend is explained almost completely by movements in two commodity groups alone, light industrial goods and natural resources, whereas in U.S.S.R.-WEST exchange the trend in heavy industrial goods also plays a significant role.

Regarding the commodity composition of exports, Figures 7-4 and 7-6 show extremely rapid period to period increases in the share of capital intensive producers' goods and natural resources. The lower panels of these figures reveal that upward trends in both heavy industrial goods and natural resources, and reciprocal declines in light industrial and agricultural good shares of exports account for the increased average capital intensity of Soviet exports to the CMEA and the WEST. Thus East-West political differences notwithstanding, the same basic changes in the commodity structure of U.S.S.R.-WORLD trade goods operate in U.S.S.R.-CMEA and U.S.S.R.-WEST exchange; an increased consumers' goods share in imports, and an increased producers' good share in exports.

Two points, however, require additional comment. First, the rate of change in the trend towards consumers' goods specialization in imports and producers' goods specialization in exports is greater in U.S.S.R.-CMEA and U.S.S.R.-WEST trade than in U.S.S.R.-WORLD exchange, which mirrors our factor proportions findings in Chapter 4. Second, in Chapter 5 we noted that natural resources

110

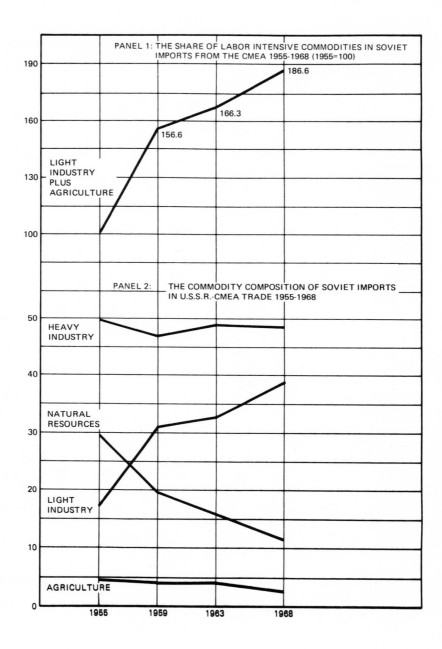

Figure 7-3. The Embodied Factor and Commodity Composition of Soviet Imports from the CMEA 1955-1968.

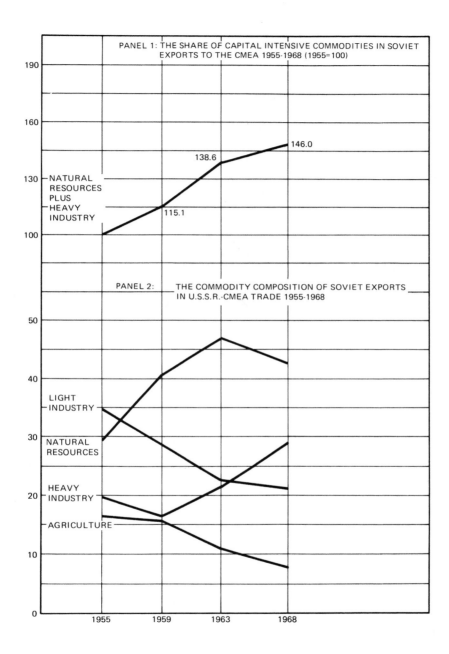

Figure 7-4. The Embodied Factor and Commodity Composition of Soviet Exports to the CMEA 1955-1968.

112

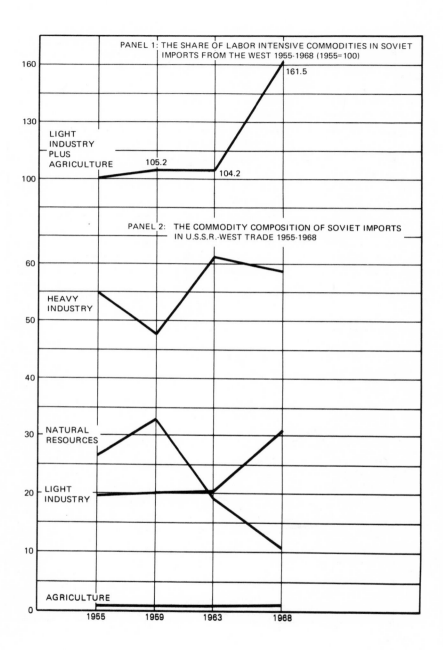

Figure 7-5. The Embodied Factor and Commodity Composition of Soviet Imports from the West 1955-1968.

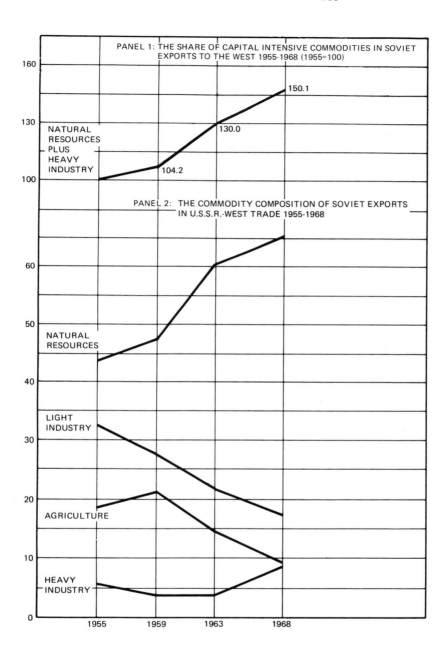

Figure 7-6. The Embodied Factor and Commodity Composition of Soviet Exports to the WEST 1955-1968.

might play a special role as a third factor in U.S.S.R.-WEST trade. A comparison, however, of Figures 7-3 and 7-5, along with 7-4 and 7-6 reveals that natural resource trends in U.S.S.R.-CMEA and U.S.S.R.-WEST trade are quite similar, the difference in factor proportions patterns being attributable more to fluctuations in the heavy industrial than in the natural resources component.

C. The Relationship Between Soviet Factor Proportions Generated in U.S.S.R.-LDC Exchange and Transformations in the Commodity Composition of Soviet Traded Goods

Soviet trade policy with the LDC contrasts markedly with the U.S.S.R.-WORLD, U.S.S.R.-CMEA, and U.S.S.R.-WEST patterns. Table 7-5 and Figures 7-7 and 7-8 show a more or less random fluctuation in the commodity composition of Soviet traded goods with the LDC. The only clearly discernible trend appears to be a modest substitution of natural resource for heavy industrial exports. Otherwise throughout the period 1955-1968 the composition of Soviet imports from the LDC remains concentrated in consumers' goods, primarily light industrial commodities, while exports are concentrated in capital intensive producers' goods, that is the heavy industrial and natural resource groups. This combination of light industrial imports and capital

Table 7-5

The Commodity Composition of Soviet Traded Goods in U.S.S.R.-LDC Exchange 1955-1968

I. Imports

Commodity Group	Commodity Group Shares of Soviet Imports from the LDC in Percentages			
	1955	1959	1963	1968
1. Natural Resources	8.8	3.4	18.0	5.2
2. Heavy Industry	1.7	1.0	3.1	2.0
3. Light Industry	78.2	85.0	55.2	86.4
4. Agriculture	11.3	10.6	23.7	6.4

II. Exports

Commodity Group	Commodity Group Shares of Soviet Exports to the LDC in Percentages			
	1955	1959	1963	1968
1. Natural Resources	23.6	15.7	37.2	37.5
2. Heavy Industry	65.7	65.5	53.7	54.1
3. Light Industry	8.2	12.9	8.8	8.3
4. Agriculture	2.4	5.9	0.2	0.1

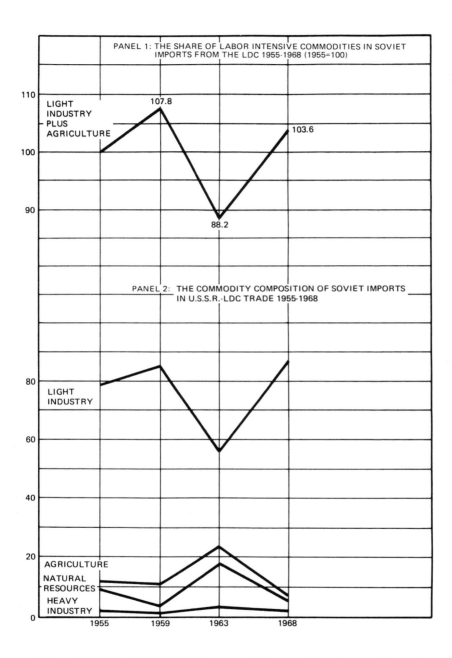

Figure 7-7. The Embodied Factor and Commodity Composition of Soviet Imports from the LDC 1955-1968.

116

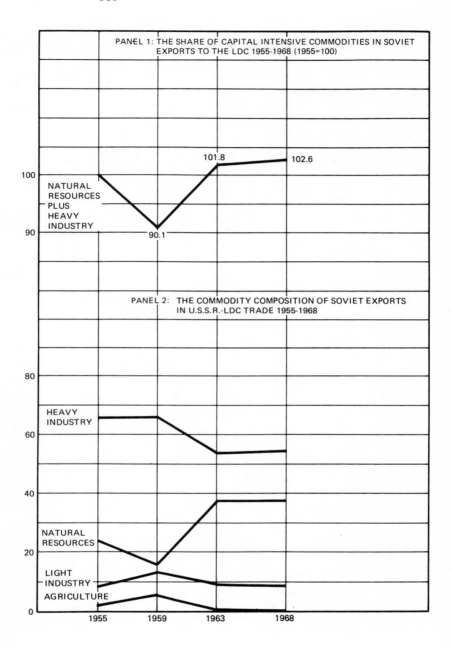

Figure 7-8. The Embodied Factor and Commodity Composition of Soviet Exports to the LDC 1955-1968.

intensive exports accounts for the extreme capital intensive export bias of U.S.S.R.-LDC factor proportion statistics.

From the international trade policy perspective, our brief survey of Soviet commodity composition trends reveals that from the beginning of the Khrushchevian period the Soviets have practiced a dual course in bilateral exchange. The composition of Soviet trade with the relatively developed countries of the CMEA and WEST has grown increasing specialized in consumers' goods imports and producers' goods (including natural resources) exports, while U.S.S.R.-LDC, already strongly specialized in precisely this way, preserved the initial composition of traded goods despite random fluctuations.[5] Moreover, we have been able to demonstrate how these trends in commodity composition are compatible with associated trends in Soviet factor proportion statistics, and why Soviet Leontief Statistics for the developed nations have tended to converge towards the Leontief Statistic values generated in U.S.S.R.-LDC trade.

Part IV
False Prices and the Factor Proportions Structure of Soviet International Trade

8

False Prices, Comparative Advantage and the Factor Proportions Structure of Soviet International Trade

The correlation discerned in the preceding chapter between trends in the commodity pattern of Soviet international trade and the structure of embodied Soviet factor proportions, revealing as it is, still nevertheless cannot be considered as an adequate economic explanation of observed results. What is missing is the establishment of a plausible mechanism which explains how Soviet planners systematically arrange the commodity composition of traded goods so that Soviet Leontief Statistics are semi-logarithmically correlated with the per capita GNP of its trading partners. Several possibilities can be entertained ranging from perfect planning, to the semi-divine intervention of Stalin's not too invisible hand. In this chapter attention is focused on what the author believes to be the least implausible of a wide variety of implausible explanations of the Heckscher-Ohlin rationality of Soviet foreign trade. Specifically, after sorting through the available alternatives, it appears that the Soviet results are the outcome of comparative advantage, labor value, accounting price calculations. The use of the term comparative advantage here should not lead the reader astray. It is neither being maintained, nor implied that the Soviet trade decision making process is efficient from a normative point of view. As we shall see labor value accounting prices do not yield the same results as Walrasian prices in determining the factor and commodity pattern of Soviet international trade. Comparative advantage in the present context refers strictly to a logical construct where relative prices serve as the principle indicator of nominally advantageous exchange. Nevertheless we will demonstrate that even in this delimited sense, the comparative advantage criterion is sufficient to generate the observed pattern of Soviet Leontief Statistics.

To appreciate the precise nature of the argument being put forth let us briefly consider the modern opportunity cost version of the traditional Ricardian comparative advantage doctrine. Given a set of prices π_ϱ/π_h representing international commodity transformation and substitution possibilities for heavy (q_h) and light (q_ϱ) industrial goods, the direction of trade will depend on the relationship between domestic and international factor cost based price relatives, assuming internationally homogeneous tastes, and technology. For example, in Figure 8-1 where domestic price relatives viewed as product transformation supply prices are π_ϱ^s/π_h^s, and their international price counterpart interpreted as commodity substitution demand prices are π_ϱ^d/π_h^d, through a dynamic Marshallian excess price quantity adjustment process:

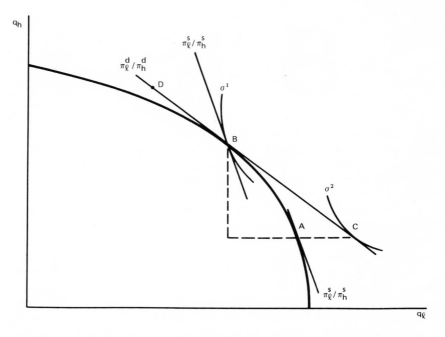

Figure 8-1. Comparative Price Advantage and the Composition of Soviet Foreign Trade.

$$\frac{dq_h}{dt} = \Theta \frac{(\pi_{\ell}^d - \pi_{\ell}^s)}{\pi_h^d \qquad \pi_h^d} \tag{8.1}$$

where:

$$\frac{\pi_{\ell}^s}{\pi_h^s} > \frac{\pi_{\ell}^d}{\pi_h^d}$$

heavy industrial production will be expanded and light industrial production diminished to accord with conditions of international demand.[1] Heavy industrial production will continue to increase up to point *B* where:

$$\frac{dq_h}{dt} = 0 \tag{8.2}$$

and

$$\frac{\pi_\varrho^s}{\pi_h^s} = \frac{\pi_\varrho^d}{\pi_h^d} \tag{8.3}$$

The augmented supply of heavy industrial goods of course will not be consumed internally. Instead heavy industrial goods will be exported in exchange for light industrial goods along the international terms of trade line π_ϱ^d/π_h^d from B to C where social welfare is maximized in its Paretian form at the tangency of the Scitovsky community indifference contour σ^2 and the international production transformation line.

The analytical significance of this result is profoundly contingent upon the principles of price formation upon which it rests. If domestic supply relatives $\pi_\varrho^s/\pi_\varrho^s$ fully reflect domestic opportunity costs and the domestic structure of aggregate demand, then they will possess the familiar welfare properties of competitive Walrasian market auction prices. Suppose, however, that domestic supply prices are formed on the basis of a different set of principles. Insofar as these principles permit parametric price formation, price relatives can still be described in terms of a negatively sloped vector in two space. The economic meaning of these prices will depend on the price formation criteria adopted. To the extent, however, that they diverge from their Walrasian correlatives without being predicated on explicit welfare principles of the Bergsonian sort, they will likewise diverge from the Paretian welfare standard embodied in Walrasian prices. Let us call this class of non-Walrasian prices, false prices, in order to underscore the point that although they may accurately characterize the real state of the system, they do not possess the clear welfare significance of their Walrasian analogues.

The importance of the distinction between false and Walrasian prices in the context of international trade depends on the extent to which international opportunity costs govern the production point and consumer's preferences govern the consumption point. If, to facilitate the exposition, we assume that false domestic prices guide the system directors regarding domestic rates of commodity substitution, then the actual trade solution will lie either to the right or the left of the Walrasian point C in Figure 8-1 depending on whether the slope of the domestic price line is either more or less steep than π_ϱ^s/π_h^s. In extreme cases, where prices are very false, the direction of trade itself may be contra-rational, giving rise to solutions such as point D in Figure 8-1 where heavy industrial goods are imported instead of exported. Worse yet, if domestic product transform occurs at any point other than B, solutions below the domestic production transformation locus are a real possibility. Clearly false prices may generate an infinite number of outcomes, all of which will conflict with the spirit of Heckscher-Ohlin theory, founded as it is on the postulates of Walrasian general equilibrium. Empirically, this means that a set of Soviet Leontief Statistics which nominally accord with Heckscher-Ohlin theory, may in fact violate the consumer's utility standard on which the theorem rests. However, to ascertain the precise extent to which the Soviet results conform with the true, Walrasian price version of Heckscher-Ohlin theory, we require detailed independent information on Soviet consumer's preferences. Needless to say, no such data exist. Although this precludes a precise assessment of the degree to which Soviet Leontief Statistics fail to embody the consumer's utility standard, the concept of false prices can still serve as a standard of evaluation in another way.

Soviet price formation is directly linked to factor costs. If factors are undervalued or overvalued according to a consistent pattern, the possibility arises that commodity prices will be regularly biased to the extent that they embody more of one or the other factor. As a consequence commodities intensively embodying the undervalued factor will appear relatively inexpensive in comparison with commodities intensively embodying the overvalued factor. If the principles of price formation function in this manner, we might anticipate seeing its empirical manifestation in the embodied factor content of Soviet trade. More precisely, we could expect Soviet trade to be undervalued factor intensive export biased in relation to its actual factor proportions availabilities. To ascertain whether this is indeed the case, let us briefly review the principles of Soviet price formation.

For ideological reasons, Soviet commodity prices are formed on the basis of the labor theory of value. Before the 1967 reforms, the time germane here, labor value accounting prices were broadly determined by average direct-plus-indirect labor costs prevailing in a particular branch of production. Indirect labor refers to the embodied labor content of material inputs and capital employed in branch production of final output. A depreciation charge was also levied.[2] As is widely understood, accounting prices of this sort diverge from their scarcity counterparts due to the omission of interest and rent charges. Capital goods as a consequence will in general be priced below their opportunity value. Moreover, the undervaluation of capital should tend to be cumulative because the value of the capital goods employed by a given branch will be understated due to an analogous omission of rent and interest charges on the capital used to produce the second generation of capital goods in question. Over time, therefore, goods produced in capital intensive industries should appear to be domestically cheap measured by prevailing accounting labor value prices.

From the viewpoint of neoclassical and Marxist labor value theory the accounting prices outlined above should be the relevant ones for determining ostensible comparative advantage.[3] However, we cannot completely rule out the possibility that an alternative set of prices might serve in this capacity. I refer here to purchasers' prices gross of turnover tax levied both on intermediate and final goods. Should Soviet planners rely on accounting prices that include these administrative charges the relative domestic undervaluation of capital intensive goods will be further exacerbated since during the period in question approximately 70 percent of all turnover tax was levied on labor as opposed to capital intensive goods. Thus, we find that the accounting practices underlying Soviet price formation conduce to make capital intensive goods appear relatively cheap, and labor intensive goods relatively dear domestically.

The fact that capital intensive goods measured with false prices are domestically cheap in comparison with Walrasian capital intensive goods prices, however, cannot determine the pattern of Soviet foreign trade in and of itself. From the perspective of international exchange relative domestic dearness, or cheapness is meaningful only in comparison with the ruling international terms of trade line illustrated in Figure 8-1. The Efimov purchasing power parity relatives shed light on this important issue. Partitioning Soviet output into two categories producers' goods and consumers' goods, which accord roughly with the capital intensive, labor intensive distinction relevant in Heckscher-Ohlin analysis, the Efimov relatives indicate that in terms of Soviet accounting prices, producers' goods are relatively less expensive than consumers' goods in comparison with international prices. Consequently, according to the principle of comparative advantage, Soviet prices signal the system directors to export capital intensive producers' goods in exchange for labor intensive consumers' goods. Strictly interpreted, remembering that Soviet international ruble prices are essentially an average of Western market prices, nominal comparative advantage not only directs the Soviets to export capital intensive goods to the LDC and CMEA, but to the WEST as well. Any other pattern could only be justified by special circumstances which would make the effective terms of trade in some foreign country diverge from effective international relatives. It should be clear, in accordance with the postulates of Heckscher-Ohlin theory that price divergences of this sort will in fact be pervasive before complete factor price equilibrium prevails internationally. It is precisely these price divergences which allow a nation to trade profitably with various foreign nations whose factor proportions are both greater and less than its own. Therefore, as a practical matter in the Heckscher-Ohlin context we would expect the Soviets to export labor intensive goods and import capital intensive goods from countries possessing more abundant relative capital availabilities. Indeed, our study has borne favorably on this very conjecture. Where domestic relatives falsely understate producers' goods cost, however, the presumption must be that relative prices will favor labor intensive Soviet exports to the WEST less often than could be anticipated if Walrasian auctioneer prices ruled. This deduction suggests a testable null hypothesis: the embodied factor proportions pattern of Soviet foreign trade does not exhibit capital intensive export biases in bilateral exchange between the Soviet Union and countries relatively more abundantly endowed with capital.

To ascertain whether the empirical evidence confirms or refutes this null hypothesis consider Figures 4-7—4-9 once again. Since theory at this point is not a perfect guide, in testing the null hypothesis we seek only to discover whether observed bilateral Soviet Leontief Statistics are distributed in the capital intensive export bias quadrant, that is, quadrant IV. Over the entire period 1955-68, on average, Figure 4-7 reveals that the null hypothesis is validated. No observations appear in quadrant IV, indicating that the Soviets do not export relatively capital intensive goods to countries that are relatively capital rich. If false labor value prices prompt the system directors to export an excessively capital intensive bundle of goods to the WEST there is no visible evidence of it. U.S.S.R.-WEST Leontief Statistics are clearly compatible with Walrasian auctioneer price expectations in the aggregate, even if prices fail to conform to the consumer's utility standard in a more detailed way. However, the average values belie the trend. Figure 4-2 demonstrates that between 1955 and 1968 U.S.S.R.-WEST trade becomes steadily less labor intensive export biased, until in 1968 the labor bias is transformed into a substantial capital intensive export bias. U.S.S.R.-CMEA exchange follows the same pattern. By 1968 Figure 4-7 reveals Soviet trade is capital intensive export biased with 5 of its 13 trade partners; five Soviet Leontief Statistics fall in quadrant IV. The null hypothesis is no longer sustainable. The new pattern of U.S.S.R.-WEST trade in the aggregate now conforms with false price, labor value comparative advantage, rather than Walrasian principles. Moreover, comparison of Figures 4-7 and 4-9 reveals a decisive increase in the capital intensive export biases generated in U.S.S.R.-CMEA trade from average, 1955-68 Soviet Leontief Statistic values, and those for 1968 alone. Pending a more cogent interpretation, the least implausible explanation of the empirical data at hand appears to suggest that the Soviets have relied on false labor value prices as a guide to trade decision making in a much more profound way than is commonly understood. For a variety of reasons, some economic, some technical and some political, false price signals were overridden as expediency dictated in the early years of this study, but over time the impact of these external criteria has diminished in importance relative to false price comparative advantage, so that in the most recent period we have clear evidence of the global capital intensive export bias anticipated on the basis of our false price hypothesis. Although the evidence is really insufficient to draw anything but a tentative conclusion, the persistence of the Leontief Statistic trends discovered in this study into the future will serve as a fundamental test of our false price comparative advantage conjecture. Validation will not only illuminate the deeper significance of our Heckscher-Ohlin theorem I findings, but should lead to a reassessment of the whole question of rational foreign trade planning under Soviet socialism.

9 Conclusion

In the preceding chapters we have explored several diverse themes. The time has now come to summarize our findings, and appraise their total significance.

The primary objective of this book has been to evaluate the rationality of Soviet international trade from the perspective of Heckscher-Ohlin theory. Utilizing the 1959 Soviet input-output table, and conventional input-output methodology, the quantitative evidence required for an assessment of the Heckscher-Ohlin theorem I rationality of Soviet trade was generated. This consisted essentially of a massive array of statistics measuring the embodied factor proportions content of normalized bundles of Soviet import replacements and exports. Both neoclassical and non-neoclassical factors were considered. To test the Heckscher-Ohlin theorem I rationality of our findings, we correlated bilateral Soviet Leontief Statistics with a per capita GNP proxy for the factor availability proportions of each particular Soviet trading partner. The resulting fit was semi-logarithmic, a specification which was shown to be compatible with a Cobb-Douglas production function in the neoclassical factor case. Econometric and graphical analysis revealed that over the entire period 1955-68 Soviet Leontief Statistics were highly and significantly correlated with our per capita GNP proxy for capital-labor availabilities. In every case where the Soviets traded with relatively low per capita income countries a capital intensive export bias was recorded. In the obverse case labor intensive export biased observations occurred. Since this behavior accords perfectly with Heckscher-Ohlin predictions, our quantitative evidence strongly suggested that Soviet foreign trade was rational measured by the Heckscher-Ohlin theorem I standard.

Further analysis, however, was contraindicative. In particular a long run trend towards global capital intensive export biased trade was detected. The results for 1968 were extremely instructive in this regard, revealing as they did that 38 percent of all Soviet Leontief Statistic observations from the Heckscher-Ohlin viewpoint fell incorrectly in the capital intensive export bias quadrant of the Leontief Statistic space.

In order to interpret these conflicting indications of the Heckscher-Ohlin theorem I rationality of Soviet international trade we explored non-neoclassical factor alternatives. Although some interesting points were uncovered, the problem remained essentially unresolved. An analysis of the commodity pattern of Soviet trade, however, demonstrated that the observed structure of Soviet Leontief Statistics corresponded with a relatively simple transformation in foreign trade commodity structure. Both in U.S.S.R.-CMEA and in U.S.S.R.-

WEST exchange, imports of labor intensive light industrial goods increased, at the same time the capital intensive heavy industrial and natural resource share of Soviet exports expanded. If there was a special, socialist pattern of trade with the CMEA, it wasn't apparent in the data. This meant that import and export trends reinforced each other in causing an intensification in the capital bias of Soviet exports to all developed countries. Moreover as was noted the commodity composition of Soviet trade with all Blocs tended to merge suggesting that a common policy was being applied in determining the commodity structure of Soviet foreign trade. This raised the possibility that considerations of a political sort might lie behind the ostensible Heckscher-Ohlin theorem I rationality of our results. For example, the incipient Soviet consumer revolution might have prompted the system directors to import an increasingly large share of consumers' goods from all sources to satisfy the burgeoning demand which could not be met from domestic supplies. While a policy of this kind may well have contributed to the observed Leontief Statistic pattern, reflection shows that it is hardly an adequate explanation of the strong semi-logarithmic fit between Soviet Leontief values and the per capita GNP of the Soviet Union's bilateral trading partners. There is simply no apparent logical connection between consumerism in general and the remarkably regular cross-sectional pattern of bilateral Soviet Leontief Statistics. The real solution appears to lie elsewhere in the mechanism of foreign trade decision making.

As the least implausible of a variety of implausible explanations, we conjectured that the Soviet Leontief Statistic pattern on average and over time is explicable in terms of false price, labor value comparative advantage. If the Soviets utilize direct-plus-indirect labor value in the formation of domestic price relatives, we demonstrated they will tend to export capital intensive goods on balance not just to the LDC and the CMEA, but to the WEST as well. We suggested that, in the 1950s various political and economic encumbrances to East-West trade restricted the full implementation of the false price comparative advantage criterion. As barriers to trade have fallen, however, labor value comparative advantage appears to have become more potent, resulting in the global capital intensive export bias predicted by our false price analysis. Final validation of this hypothesis must await further empirical study, but if we are correct then our Heckscher-Ohlin theorem I results fall into place. Comparative advantage calculations, albeit of a special sort, are seen to govern the commodity pattern of Soviet foreign trade. The false labor value prices utilized to calculate nominal comparative advantage understate the opportunity cost of capital intensive producers' goods. As a consequence, the embodied factor proportions content of Soviet commodity trade tends to be capital intensive export biased. The extent of this bias depends, as theory suggests, on the price terms offered by each Soviet trading partner. Where trade occurs between two relatively developed nations the false Soviet producers' goods price advantage is small in comparison to Soviet terms of exchange with the less developed countries.

Consequently, relatively small capital intensive export biases characterize Soviet trade with the developed nations, in contrast to the high intensity capital bias values recorded with the less developed countries. False price comparative advantage therefore accounts both for the direction of the observed capital intensive biases, and their relative magnitude. In short, it explains the Soviet Leontief Statistic pattern for the later years of our study.

The Heckscher-Ohlin theorem I rationality of the average Soviet Leontief Statistic structure 1955-68 is also explicable in false price perspective, if we accept the premise that the influence of false prices on the commodity pattern of Soviet trade in the 1950s was modified by exogenous economic and political factors. False prices in this case account for the ordered Heckscher-Ohlin theorem I rational pattern of Soviet Leontief Statistics while exogenous factors suppress the emergence of a capital intensive export bias.

Clearly, from a logical point of view the false price hypothesis can serve as a rational cement binding the diverse aspects of our empirical findings together. In the final analysis, however, whether our false comparative advantage conjecture is correct or not, the overall Heckscher-Ohlin theorem I rationality of Soviet international trade cannot be gainsayed. Except for normative considerations which lie beyond conventional measurement, and the recently emergent global capital intensive export bias, the basic embodied factor proportions structure of Soviet trade stands as a major analytical challenge to all students of comparative economic systems.

The magnitude of the Soviet achievement in this regard is best perceived in comparison with analogous American results. Although few can doubt that American market prices reflect opportunity costs more effectively than Soviet accounting prices, repeated tests of the macroeconomic Heckscher-Ohlin theorem I rationality of American foreign trade have proved disappointing. In most cases the embodied factor proportions content of American trade has actually been the reverse of the Heckscher-Ohlin rational pattern. Empirical and analytical attempts to quantitatively and qualitatively adjust the basic American Leontief Statistic findings to better conform with Heckscher-Ohlin expectations have succeeded only in minimal ways. Thus the contradiction: the relatively micro efficient American economic system has proven to be relatively macroeconomically irrational judged by Heckscher-Ohlin theorem I, while the relatively micro-inefficient Soviet system appears macroeconomically rational evaluated on the same criterion. The clear implication of this highly paradoxical situation is that the relative merit of alternative economic systems cannot be superficially extrapolated from their theoretical characteristics alone. More penetrating analytic tools will have to be developed, along the lines elaborated recently by Janos Kornai,[1] before we can confidently maintain that the behavior of alternative real world economic systems is adequately encompassed in complete, predictive models.

The dearth of real, concrete systems analysis at present ultimately imparts a degree of ambiguity to the deeper significance of our study. Suppose, for example, that American foreign trade is macroeconomically rational in a world where the postulates of Heckscher-Ohlin theory fail to hold in any consistent way. Should we then deduce that the Heckscher-Ohlin theorem I rationality of Soviet foreign trade has been achieved by over zealous attention to nominal as opposed to real comparative advantage? No answer to this rhetorical question is at hand. But the problem will undoubtedly repay further research.

Alternatively, suppose the macroeconomic rationality of Soviet foreign trade is real enough. How should the Soviets go about correcting the capital intensive export bias tendency which has emerged in the 1960s? Several alternatives exist. The adjusted factor cost standard might be adopted in the formation of domestic prices, bringing prices more closely in line with scarcity values. Alternatively, if the system directors believe that true opportunity costs are adequately reflected in a two factor neoclassical model, using Leontief techniques they might compute the embodied factor proportions of various alternative foreign trade plan variants, selecting the one which is most Heckscher-Ohlin theorem I rational. In this way embodied factor proportions can serve as a surrogate for opportunity cost pricing. Whether the Soviet system directors would really want to follow such a procedure will depend ultimately on their assessment of the correct determinants of profitable international exchange.

Whatever the final outcome in this regard, the related problems of systems specificity and the real opportunity costs suggest that the ultimate significance of this book must await additional empirical research. For the present we content ourselves with having demonstrated that during the period 1955-68 the embodied factor proportions of Soviet international trade viewed in the aggregate was astonishing consistent with the pure Heckscher-Ohlin theoretical standard, and that this macroeconomic rationality has a plausible comparative advantage interpretation. Furthermore our findings suggest that the false labor value prices used to measure comparative advantage have tended recently to make the embodied factor proportions content of Soviet foreign trade Heckscher-Ohlin capital intensive export biased. To overcome this problem the Soviets must either abandon false labor value accounting prices in their comparative advantage calculations, or devise ancillary methods to ensure that the commodity composition of traded goods accurately reflects ruling opportunity costs. Despite this difficulty, our analysis on balance has revealed that Soviet foreign trade planning has been capable and will continue to be capable of achieving surprisingly Heckscher-Ohlin consistent macroeconomic results. Whether the Soviet version of Heckscher-Ohlin consistency will prove to be the most desirable standard of economic merit, however, still remains an open empirical question.

Appendixes

Appendix A:
A Consistent International Comparison of National Income in 15 Countries Valued in 1967 Dollars and Computed on a Purchasing Power Parity Basis

Although the computation of national income data for international comparison is an ambiguous exercise due both to conceptual and computational difficulties, I have attempted to compute a consistent national income series based on the purchasing power parity concept which should be acceptable for the restricted purposes of our study. The details of the calculations made for each particular bloc of countries considered are given below.

A. Western Countries

Data for the computation of Western per capita GNP values in 1967 dollars comes from *National Accounts of OECD Countries, 1950-1968*. Initially, national income figures are available in a series calculated in current dollars and current exchange rates. To conform with the calculations of per capita income for non-Western countries OECD national price deflators are used to convert the series to a 1955 base. In addition, devaluations and appreciations of national currencies vis-à-vis the U.S. dollar occurring after 1955 are eliminated through deflation since adjustments in international exchange rates are typically the result of price level inflation which is accounted for by using constant 1955 prices to measure per capita real income over time. Dollar values of the real national income of Western countries in domestic currency values for the OECD series were obtained through conversion with the exchange rate prevailing in 1955. These dollar values are adjusted to the geometric mean of Milton Gilbert's purchasing power parity calculations for each Western country by coefficients presented in Simon Kuznets, *Modern Economic Growth*, p. 376, taken from the original source.[1] Finally, the geometric mean purchasing power parity series in 1955 dollars is adjusted to a 1967 dollar basis with the aid of the dollar price index found in the OECD source.

B. Less Developed Countries

The key source for the computation of the real national income of the less developed countries is *National Accounts of Less Developed Countries*

Table A-1
Per Capita GNP in 1967 Dollars, With Constant 1955 Exchange Rate, Adjusted
to a Geometric Mean Purchasing Power Basis

Country	Average	Year 1955	1957	1959	1963	1965	1968
U.S.	3513	3145		3195	3487		4226
WEST	1937	1562		1748	2044		2395
United Kingdom	2094	1821		1970	2164		2424
West Germany	2093	1588		1897	2234		2652
France	1906	1493		1672	2010		2450
Finland	1655	1346		1453	1769		2052
CMEA[a]	1052	798		952	1096		1363
Czechoslovakia	1536	1198		1456	1576		1912
East Germany	1412	1041		1358	1500		1748
U.S.S.R.	1278	975		1182	1309		1649
Hungary	1011	787		888	1062		1308
Poland	883	715		792	899		1124
Rumania	741	564		612	764		1024
Bulgaria	731	485		606	773		1061
LDC[b]	244	198		225	257		262
UAR	319	252		299	348		357
China	190		190			190	
India	157	144		150	166		166

[a]CMEA excludes the U.S.S.R.
[b]LDC excludes China. If China is included the average per capita GNP is 224.

1950-1966, which presents a population and real product series 1950-66 for the
UAR and India. The UAR real product series is in domestic currency, measuring
net domestic product at factor cost with a 1954 base. The India series also in
domestic prices has a 1960 base and measures gross domestic product in market
prices. Since both series terminate in 1966, to obtain 1968 estimates I
extrapolate from 1966 real product values using a real per capita product growth
rate series 1957-59/1964-66. I next compute per capita real product values in
domestic currencies and convert these figures to dollar values with exchange
rates for 1960 provided in the OECD source. In order to make the dollar values
of the real per capita products of the less developed countries conformable with
our calculations for the Western countries, I adjust the per capita real product
series to a geometric mean purchasing power parity basis with the aid of
coefficients provided by Kuznets in *Modern Economic Growth,* p. 382. Finally,
the geometric mean purchasing power parity per capita product series is adjusted
to a 1967 U.S. dollar basis with OECD U.S. price indices.

C. China

The OECD does not supply data on Chinese national income. A survey of various available series in the specialized literature on the Chinese economy shows that there is little agreement on the magnitude of Chinese national income in yuan and still less in dollars. One point however seems clear: Chinese national income in 1965 after the Great Leap Forward was approximately equal to Chinese national income in 1957. Edwin Jones presents dollar values of Chinese GNP 1957 and 1965 without explaining their derivation.[2] The dollar values for both years are equal, conforming closely with official indices and the estimates of Western specialists on the Chinese economy. Regarding the dollar magnitudes, I made a rough check by converting official figures to dollars with the 1952 official conversion rate and obtained a value of 74.7 dollars per capita. When adjusted to 1965 dollars, Official Chinese per capita GNP is estimated at 96.6 dollars, a value similar to Jones figure of 101 dollars. It seems clear that Jones made his calculations on the basis of data which corresponded closely with official statistics. Yuan-Li Wu in *The Economy of Communist China*, p. 170, informs us that if the cross rate between the Hong Kong dollar and the U.S. dollar is 5.5, a rate of 2.35 yuan per U.S. dollar would be obtained. Since the official 1952 exchange rate is 2.343 the Jones estimate may not be totally unacceptable, and will accordingly be used in this study.

D. Eastern Europe

The computation of a per capita national income series in dollars for the Eastern European countries is based on data published by Thad Alton.[3] Alton presents an extension of Maurice Ernst purchasing power parity series (Table 4, p. 49) in 1967 dollars. The original series used a 1955 base and was computed in two stages. First, GNP at current prices were converted to Deutschmarks by means of purchasing power ratios, which were then adjusted to take into account the alternative purchasing power option of converting West German magnitudes into East European currencies. Second, East European GNP figures in adjusted Deutschmarks were converted to dollars using the geometric means of the two sets of dollar values in purchasing power equivalents for 1955 as estimated for the OEEC by Milton Gilbert and Associates.[4]

Alton also gives us in Table 1 (p. 46) growth indices for all Eastern European countries with a 1955 base. To compute a per capita national income series in 1967 prices I therefore adjusted Alton's per capita GNP figures for 1967 (Table 4, p. 49) based on the geometric mean purchasing power parity computation, by his growth rate series, and Paul Myers population series.[5] This yields a per capita GNP series based on the geometric mean of the Gilbert purchasing power parity study that is fully analogous with our series for Western Europe.

E. Soviet Union

The Soviet per capita national income series in 1967 prices was computed by first taking the geometric mean of Bergson's purchasing power parity calculations for 1955,[6] and computing the dollar value of U.S.S.R. GNP in 1955 using OECD data on U.S. GNP in current 1955 dollars. This Soviet GNP figure in 1955 dollars was then used as a base for the computation of a real national income series in dollars by applying Stanley Cohn's growth index 1950-1969.[7] Next the national income series was adjusted to a per capita basis using Soviet population statistics.[8] Finally, the per capita GNP series was converted to 1967 dollars with the aid of the OECD price index for the U.S.

Appendix B:
Bilateral Commodity
Balances and Sectoral
Factor Proportions

The Heckscher-Ohlin theorem I postulates a relationship between the ratio of factor proportions embodied in competitive import replacements and exports, and factor availabilities. This hypothesis can be empirically verified simply by showing that a set of Leontief Statistics generated in trade with countries possessing different relative factor supplies is positively correlated with the capital labor availabilities ratio, and that the observations lie in the first and third quadrants of a set of axes drawn through the hypothetical point where the domestic nation trades with itself. The theory as usually conceived in neoclassical input and output aggregates fails to explicitly specify whether the bilateral commodity balances (net imports or exports) of each sector will be correlated with factor availabilities. The spirit of the Heckscher-Ohlin theorem which stresses that commodity prices are basically determined by factor cost suggests that the factor proportions characterizing any given industry will strongly influence its international competitiveness. If factor proportions do indeed determine the international competitiveness of the various sectors we would expect to find empirical evidence for the hypothesis by studying the correlation between net exports (exports minus imports) and the direct-plus-indirect capital labor ratio of each sector.[1] To ascertain whether this conjecture has merit in the Soviet case, consider the scatter diagram (Figure B-1), which measures net exports on the vertical and the direct-plus-indirect capital labor on the horizontal axis. Sectors with zero entries for both imports and exports have been omitted. The observations in Figure B-1 seem to be distributed in a fairly random way, although a definite clustering of points is apparent. Since theory does not provide any real clues as to the proper functional specification relating net exports and sectoral factor proportions ratios, as a starting point I ran a regression on the following linear form for 1959:

$$X - M = \alpha + \beta \, k/l \qquad \qquad (B.1)$$

where:

X = a vector of exports

M = a vector of imports

α = a constant term

β = the coefficient of the direct-plus-indirect capital labor requirements ratio

k = a vector of direct-plus-indirect capital requirements

l = a vector of direct-plus-indirect labor requirements.

137

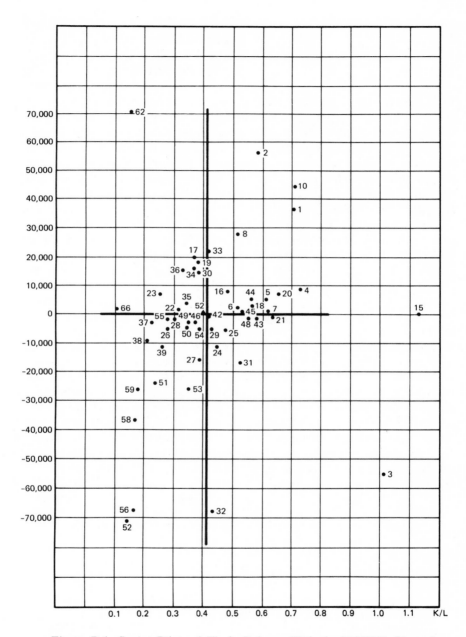

Figure B-1. Soviet Bilateral Trade Balance With the WORLD, Plotted Against Direct-Plus-Indirect Capital-Labor Requirements by Industry, in 1959.

The results favored the null hypothesis; with the $R = 0.2280$ only 5 percent of the variance in the dependent variable was explained, and even this small correlation was barely significant at the 90 percent confidence level. However, if we exclude three outliers, agriculture (62), crude petroleum (9), and nonferrous ores (3) as special cases, the fit is greatly improved. A regression run with these three observations deleted yielded an R of 0.4734, with a positive β coefficient significant at the 0.995 level, explaining 22 percent of the variance in the dependent variable. The analogous test run for 1968 net export generated similar results, with somewhat reduced explanatory power. The R was 0.3888 and the positive β coefficient was significant at the 0.99 level, accounting for 15 percent of the variance in the dependent variable. Although these findings are not spectacular they do indicate a tendency for net exports to be linearly and positively correlated with sectoral factor proportions.

Figure B-1 affords us some additional insights. If we draw a set of coordinate axes through the point representing average sector direct-plus-indirect capital labor proportions (excluding the three outliers) and the zero net export line, we can establish the location of an equilibrium point where factor proportions favor neither imports or exports. Observations falling in quadrants I and III are consistent with the hypothesis that bilateral commodity balances have a tendency to be positively correlated with sector factor proportions, while those falling in quadrants II and IV manifest an opposing tendency. Figure B-1 shows that a majority of observations (71 percent) are located in quadrants I and III. Moreover, the computed regression line passes reasonably near the origin of the coordinate axes revealing that not only does the positive correlation between net exports and sector factor proportions exist, but that in a modest way, it is consistent with the spirit of the Heckscher-Ohlin approach.

No conclusive theoretical deductions can be drawn from the evidence at hand, but it will be interesting to observe whether factor proportions studies for other countries confirm our findings of a tendency for net sectoral imports and net sectoral exports to be positively correlated with sector factor proportions. If Baldwin's results are indicative however the evidence will not be clear-cut. His American findings demonstrate a negative, rather than the desired positive correlation.[2]

Appendix C:
Soviet Leontief Statistics
with the Influence of
Agriculture Removed

The material contained in the following pages was initially part of the main body of the text, but since subsequent analysis demonstrated that agriculture plays a very subsidiary part in determining the structure of Soviet factor proportions it was removed and placed in this Appendix. In deciding to preserve a section on the role of agriculture in the determination of Soviet factor proportions even in Appendix form, I was motivated by the following considerations. First, agriculture has traditionally been considered a sector governed by very special factors in the Soviet context. Second, some analysts prefer to lump agriculture together with natural resources in analyzing the independent effect of natural resources on the structure of a nation's Leontief Statistics. The inclusion of this section will enable those who hold this viewpoint to ascertain Soviet factor proportions behavior when agricultural and natural resource influences are removed simultaneously. Finally, there exists some sentiment that agriculture functions in a special capacity under American conditions, so that the material contained here on the Soviet experience can be used for comparative purposes in weighing the international significance of agriculture viewed as a third factor.

Studies of American factor proportions have shown that the agricultural sector imparts a significant labor intensive export bias to U.S. commodity trade. Baldwin found that the deletion of the agricultural vector caused the U.S. Leontief Statistic to rise 1.4 bias units from 1.27 to 1.41.[1] Since the Soviet agrarian sector has long been subject to special governmental consideration, one would anticipate that, like its American counterpart, removing the influence of the agricultural vector might strongly affect Soviet factor proportions. Table C-1 and Figures C-1 and C-2 all bear on this issue. Row 1 of Table C-1 presents Soviet Leontief Statistics generated in U.S.S.R.-WORLD trade for various years. The average value 1955-1968 is 0.8017, which when compared with its all sector equivalent of 0.8681 reveals a decline of 0.95 bias units. This means that the deletion of the agricultural vector causes a substantially increased capital intensive export bias. Since the removal of agricultural influence causes the American Leontief Statistic to rise 1.40 bias units, the Soviet result may appear paradoxical, in view of the fact that the agricultural sector is a relatively labor intensive activity in both countries. However, the ostensible contradiction is easily explained by the fact that agriculture is a net import commodity in the United States and a net export item in the Soviet Union. The deletion of the agricultural vector raises the average export capital-labor ratio more than the import capital-labor ratio in the Soviet case causing the Leontief Statistic to fall.

141

Table C-1

Soviet Leontief Statistics Generated in Trade Between the U.S.S.R. and 13 Other Countries in the Years 1955, 1959, 1963, 1968 With the Influence of the Agricultural Vector (62) Deleted

U.S.S.R. Trade Pattern With	Soviet Leontief Statistics (65 Sectors) Year				
	1955	1959	1963	1968	1955-1968
1. WORLD	0.9573	0.8144	0.7673	0.6679	0.8017
2. WEST and its components	1.3960	1.2976	1.1390	0.7946	1.1870
3. United Kingdom	1.6804	1.5806	1.5292	1.0944	1.4712
4. West Germany	1.6616	1.8387	0.9799	0.7797	1.3150
5. France	0.9959	1.1076	1.2099	0.8382	1.0379
6. Finland	1.3384	1.1602	1.0859	0.6501	1.0587
7. CMEA and its components	1.1562	0.9038	0.7192	0.6220	0.8503
8. Czechoslovakia	1.8238	0.8586	0.7599	0.6654	1.0269
9. East Germany	1.1678	1.1583	0.8130	0.8362	0.9938
10. Hungary	0.8331	0.6276	0.5702	0.5541	0.6464
11. Poland	0.9388	0.9226	0.7687	0.6458	0.8190
12. Rumania	1.1288	0.8342	0.6706	0.5645	0.7995
13. Bulgaria	0.8036	0.6215	0.5701	0.4551	0.6126
14. LDC and its components	0.5254	0.4464	0.4132	0.4100	0.4595
15. UAR	0.2754	0.2882	0.3696	0.4022	0.3339
16. China	0.5351	0.4673	0.4240	0.3593	0.4464
17. India	0.3954	0.3747	0.3959	0.4327	0.3997

Table C-2

The Decline in Soviet Leontief Statistics 1955-1968 Computed on a Full 66 Sector Basis and With Agriculture Deleted, Measured in Bias Units

U.S.S.R. Trade Pattern With	Bias Unit Decrease in Soviet Leontief Statistics 1955-1968	
	66 Sector Basis	65 Sector Basis
1. WORLD	−4.29	−5.00
2. WEST	−8.23	−7.62
3. CMEA	−7.76	−7.64
4. LDC	−0.48	−5.37

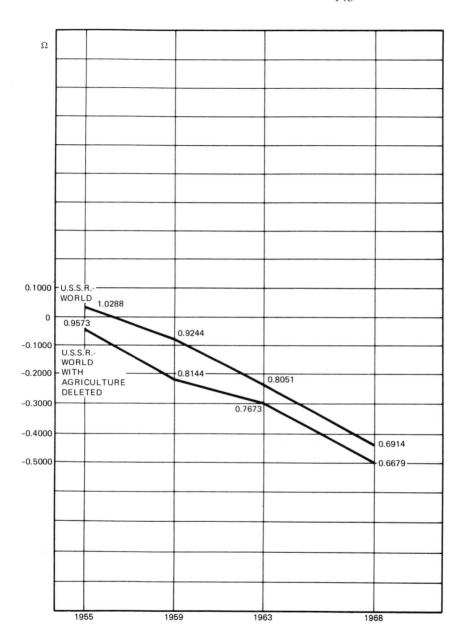

Figure C-1. Comparison of Soviet Leontief Statistics Generated in U.S.S.R.-WORLD Trade With and Without the Inclusion of the Agricultural Sector, Over the Period 1955-1968.

With agricultural imports greater than exports the deletion of the effect of the agricultural vector raises the import capital-labor ratio more than the export capital-labor ratio, yielding the opposite result in the American case. Figure C-1 demonstrates moreover that the increased capital intensiveness of Soviet exports resulting from the removal of the influence of agriculture, affects all observations similarly, but with diminishing force, thereby generating a secular trend lying below, but converging towards the U.S.S.R.-WORLD curve of Soviet Leontief Statistics with agriculture included.

If we disaggregate the U.S.S.R.-WORLD Leontief Statistics on a BLOC basis, we find in Figure C-2 that the capital intensive export bias associated with the deletion of the average influence of agriculture is sustained only for two regional aggregates, the Soviet Leontief Statistic falling 1.57 bias units in U.S.S.R.-CMEA and 2.83 bias units in U.S.S.R.-WEST trade. A similar comparison of bilateral factor proportions values generated in U.S.S.R.-LDC exchange exhibits a more complex pattern. While the average Soviet Leontief Statistic value for the period 1955-1968 with agricultural influence removed displays a less capital intensive export bias equivalent to 1.23 bias units than with the full 66 sector measure, Figure C-2 shows that in 1959 and 1963 the opposite relationship held. A glance at the U.S.S.R.-CHINA, U.S.S.R.-INDIA, and U.S.S.R.-UAR entries in Table C-1 demonstrates that conflicting factor proportion trends in the individual components of the LDC aggregate, along with a changing pattern of underlying trade share weights accounts for the less decisive U.S.S.R.-LDC result, so that we again find that the heterogeneity of the LDC observational unit makes unambiguous interpretation more difficult than in the CMEA and WEST cases. If we next consider country-by-country factor proportions for the CMEA and WEST by comparing the Leontief values in Table C-1 with Tables 4-2, 4-3, and 4-4 we find that factor proportion differentials between Leontief Statistics computed with 66 and 65 sectors are generally reflected in the U.S.S.R.-COUNTRY figures, with the U.S.S.R.-LDC case again exhibiting a disparate pattern. Thus, the deletion of the agricultural vector has a fairly homogeneous impact on the structure of Soviet Leontief Statistics, with the exception of the LDC where the impact is mixed. This fact is brought out by Figure C-3 relating average Soviet Leontief Statistics 1955-1968 to our per capita GNP proxy for underlying capital-labor availabilities. The semi-logarithmic regression line fitting the observations has shifted slightly to the southeast and the slope has declined a few degrees compared with Figure 4-7, but the overall effect is small; both distributions satisfying Heckscher-Ohlin theorem I and both yielding good fits with respective R's; 0.9614 in the full vector case, and 0.9121 with agriculture deleted.

Soviet Leontief Statistics computed on full and truncated bases are analogous in still another respect. Table C-2 shows the secular tendency towards an increasingly capital intensive export bias over the period 1955-1968. The trends for U.S.S.R.-WORLD and U.S.S.R.-BLOC based on 66 and 65 sector aggrega-

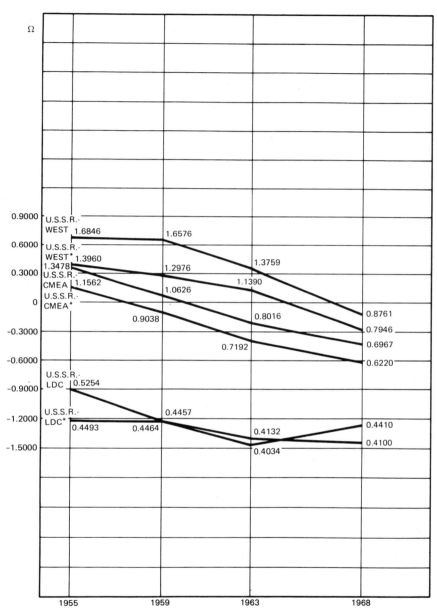

*Signifies the deletion of the agricultural sector

Figure C-2. Comparison of Trends in Soviet Leontief Statistics Generated in U.S.S.R.-Regional Trade, With and Without the Inclusion of the Agricultural Sector, Over the Period 1955-1968.

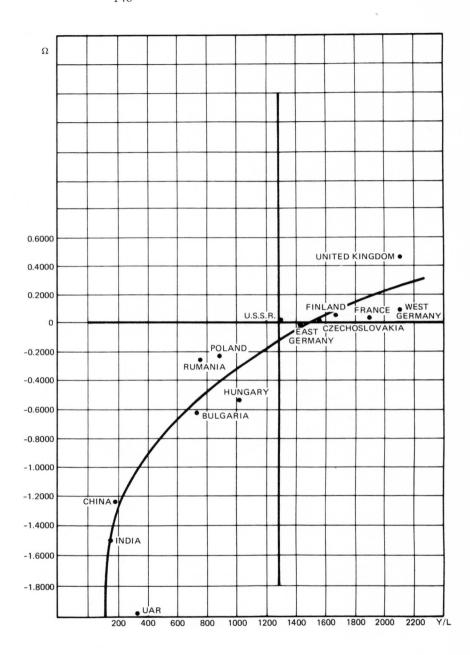

Figure C-3. Soviet Leontief Statistics With Agricultural Deleted, Average Values 1955-1968, Plotted as a Function of Per Capita GNP.

tions are strikingly similar, with the usual exception of the U.S.S.R.-LDC case. This last additional piece of evidence, taken with the other comparisons, shows conclusively that there are no special factors at work in the agricultural sector which fundamentally alter our analysis of Soviet factor proportions. The consonance between the pattern of Soviet Leontief Statistics and Heckscher-Ohlin theorem I is preserved and the validity of our neoclassical factors is not called into question. Thus, although it is interesting to note the capital intensive export bias associated with the deletion of the agricultural vector, our analysis remains fundamentally unaltered.

Appendix D:
Data Sources and Computational Procedures Used in the Calculation of a Consistent Per Capita GNP Dollar Series for 13 Areas Trading with the U.S. in 1962

The per capita GNP series in 1967 American dollars, derived and explained in Appendix A is extended here to accommodate Baldwin's country variables employed in his analysis of American Leontief Statistics.

A. Western Countries

American, Canadian, O.E.C.D. European and Japanese per capita GNP values are all computed from the series contained in *National Accounts of O.E.C.D. Countries, 1950-1968* and adjusted in accordance with the procedures utilized in Appendix A, section A, with the exception that no purchasing power parity adjustment was made in the Canadian case because of the close proximity of per capita product values in the U.S. and Canada.

B. Less Developed Countries

The definition of less developed countries in American and Soviet contexts is extremely different. The notation LDC* is used to distinguish American from Soviet LDC designations. In computing per capita GNPs for American LDC trading partners I first calculated the share of American exchange with four less developed regional groupings as they appeared in *U.S. Statistical Abstracts 1964*, pp. 876-81: North and Central America, South America, Asia, and Africa. These shares were then used on similarly defined O.E.C.D. per capita U.S. dollar GNP data for 1960 found in *National Accounts of Less Developed Countries, 1950-1966* to arrive at a weighted dollar aggregate of the per capita GNP of developing nations which trade with the United States. Other adjustments required to achieve full comparability with our earlier GNP series are in accordance with the procedures detailed in Appendix A, section B.

C. Other

The "Other" category is a very peculiar amalgam and it is difficult to appreciate why Baldwin found it useful for analytical work. Nevertheless, following his

149

methodology, we have computed a per capita GNP figure for the OTHER aggregate. Since Oceania accounts for 80 percent and the CMEA for 19 percent of the OTHER category these two groupings are treated as the total OTHER entity. A 1963 per capita GNP figure for Oceania given in U.S. dollars was taken from the U.N. publication, *Yearbook of National Account Statistics, 1969, Volume II, International Tables*, Table 1, and adjusted back to 1962 with the aid of a per capita real volume index series supplied in Table 7. The Kuznets purchasing power parity adjustment coefficients were then applied in conformity with our standardized procedure. The CMEA per capita GNP values were derived from our 1963 series, adjusted for changes in real product and population growth. For details on data sources and the computation of the per capita dollar CMEA GNP series see Appendix A, section D. Having obtained fully adjusted per capita GNP figures for Oceania and the CMEA, the per capita product for the OTHER aggregate itself was calculated simply as the weighted value of its component parts.

Table D-1

Per Capita GNP Values for 13 Countries in 1962, Computed in 1967 U.S. Dollars, Adjusted to a Geometric Mean Purchasing Power Basis

Country	GNP
U.S.	3387
Canada	2468
Other	1762
1. Oceania	1927
2. CMEA	1067
a. Czechoslovakia	1617
b. East Germany	1456
c. Hungary	1010
d. Poland	856
e. Rumania	718
f. Bulgaria	745
O.E.C.D.: Europe	1716
Japan	954
LDC*	520

Notes

Notes

Chapter 1
The Role of Factor Proportions in International Trade: Problems of Theory and Measurement

1. For example, see Judith Thornton, "Differential Capital Charges and Resource Allocation in Soviet Industry," JPE, May 1971, pp. 545-77.

2. Gottfried Haberler, A SURVEY OF INTERNATIONAL TRADE THEORY, p. 2.

3. Ibid., p. 18. For a full discussion of the conditions required for factor price equalization, see Paul Samuelson, "International Trade and the Equalization of Factor Prices," ECONOMIC JOURNAL, June 1948; and "International Factor-Price Equalization Once Again," ECONOMIC JOURNAL, June 1949. For a more recent discussion of the problem, including empirical results pertaining to these conditions, see Robert Baldwin, "Determinants of the Commodity Structure of U.S. Trade," AER, March 1971.

4. Ibid., p. 19.

5. Leontief himself calls the ratio "a" for want of a better term. See Wassily Leontief, "Factor Proportions and the Structure of American Trade: Further Theoretical and Empirical Analysis," REVIEW OF ECONOMICS AND STATISTICS, November 1956.

Chapter 2
The 1959 Soviet Input-Output Table and Other Data Sources

1. Vladimir G. Treml, INPUT-OUTPUT ANALYSIS AND SOVIET PLANNING, unpublished, 1964, p. 10.

2. Vladimir G. Treml, THE 1959 SOVIET INTERSECTORAL FLOW TABLE, VOLUME I, Research Analysis Corporation, Technical Paper RAC-TP-137, November 1964, pp. 46-54.

3. Ibid., p. 46.

4. Ibid., p. 48.

5. Ibid., p. 49.

6. Ibid., p. 53.

7. This information was confirmed by Treml in private conversations.

8. Vladimir Treml, "New Soviet Interindustry Data," in RECENT SOVIET ECONOMIC PERFORMANCE: SELECTED ASPECTS, Research Analysis Corporation, RAC-P-38, August 1968, pp. 26-28; Treml, "New Soviet Inter-Industry Data," in SOVIET ECONOMIC PERFORMANCE: 1966-67, JEC, pp.

146-47; Treml, "New Soviet Capital Data," SOVIET STUDIES, 18 (3), January 1967, pp. 290-95.

9. M.P. Eidel'man, MEZHOTRASLEVOI BALANS OBSHCHESTVEN-NOGO PRODUKTA, Moskva, 1966, pp. 207-208.

10. This information comes from private conversations with Treml.

11. Concerning the theoretical and computational difficulties associated with the capacity concept see Lawrence Klein, "Some Theoretical Issues In the Measurement of Capacity," ECONOMETRICA, 28 (April 1960), pp. 272-86.

12. See Chapter 3, Section B.

13. See Chapter 3, Section C.

14. Note that sectoral capital-labor ratios based on the observed standard will exceed those computed on a capacity standard. However, since the Leontief Statistic is a ratio of import to export capital labor ratios, the structure of unused capital stocks rather than the capital-labor ratios themselves is the decisive factor.

15. E. Iasin and M. Fidler, VESTNIK STATISTIKI, Moscow, 12, 1965, pp. 36-43.

16. See Chapter 3, Section C.

17. A. Efimov and L. Berri (eds.), METODY PLANIROVANIIA MEZHO-TRASLEVYIKH PROPORTSII, Moscow, 1965, pp. 96-97.

18. Treml, THE 1959 SOVIET INTERSECTORAL FLOW TABLE, Volume I, p. 24.

19. Ibid., pp. 59-111.

Chapter 3
The Embodied Factor Proportions Computation

1. See Vladimir Treml, "The 1959 Soviet Input-Output Table," In NEW DIRECTIONS, JEC, 1966, p. 14n. Also see Daniel Gallik, THE SOVIET FINANCIAL SYSTEM, U.S. Dept. of Commerce, p. 94.

2. Since only the Efimov price relatives were available to me, the actual computation of $(1 + \Gamma)^{-1}$ proceeded as follows:

$$(3.2n) \begin{bmatrix} \frac{1}{\mu_1 m_1/m_1^*} & & \\ & \frac{1}{\mu_2 m_2/m_2^*} & \\ & & \frac{1}{\mu_3 m_3/m_3^*} \end{bmatrix} \begin{bmatrix} \frac{\lambda_1 v_1}{v_1^*} & & \\ & \frac{\lambda_2 v_2}{v_2^*} & \\ & & \frac{\lambda_3 v_3}{v_3^*} \end{bmatrix} =$$

$$\begin{bmatrix} \frac{\lambda_1}{\mu_1} & & \\ & \frac{\lambda_2}{\mu_2} & \\ & & \frac{\lambda_3}{\mu_3} \end{bmatrix} \begin{bmatrix} \frac{v_1/v_1^*}{m_1/m_1^*} & & \\ & \frac{v_2/v_2^*}{m_2/m_2^*} & \\ & & \frac{v_3/v_3^*}{m_3/m_3^*} \end{bmatrix}$$

where: $v^* =$ exports valued in foreign trade ruble prices

$m^* =$ imports valued in foreign trade ruble prices

In Equation (3.24) we assumed that $M \approx V$, if in addition $M^* \approx V^*$, which should be true if $M \approx V$, then the diagonal commodity matrix should approximate the identity matrix, so that

$$
\begin{bmatrix}
\hat{\lambda_1/\mu_1} & & \\
& \lambda_2/\hat{\mu_2} & \\
& & \lambda_3/\hat{\mu_3}
\end{bmatrix}
\approx
\begin{bmatrix}
\lambda_1/\mu_1 & & \\
& \lambda_2/\mu_2 & \\
& & \lambda_3/\mu_3
\end{bmatrix}
$$

where the circumflexed variables are estimates of the true values.

3. Richard Moorsteen and Raymond Powell, THE SOVIET CAPITAL STOCK 1928-1962, p. 14n. Treml has confirmed this opinion for 1959.

Chapter 4
The Neoclassical Factor Proportions of
Soviet International Trade 1955-1968

1. For a full discussion of this measure see Chapter 1, Section E, and Chapter 3, Section A.

2. See Chapter 1, Section E, for an analysis of the exact meaning of this formulation.

3. The 1947 and 1962 Leontief Statistics were computed using the capital stock alone as the capital measure. The 1951 figure uses an augmented definition of capital stock plus depreciation. See Leontief, "Factor Proportions and Structure of American Trade," REVIEW OF ECONOMICS AND STATISTICS, Nov. 1956, pp. 393 and 397. The 1947 Leontief Statistic with depreciation included in the capital stock measure is 1.1757. The 1962 figure comes from Robert Baldwin, "Determinants of the Commodity Structure of U.S. Trade," AER, March 1971, p. 133.

4. The CMEA for our purposes includes only the following countries: Czechoslovakia, East Germany, Poland, Hungary, Bulgaria, and Rumania. Mongolia and Albania are excluded.

5. The WEST aggregate is composed of the United Kingdom, West Germany, France, and Finland, which on average account for 53 percent of Soviet trade with developed Western nations.

6. In Chapter 8, we discuss the precise nature of this common causal nexus.

7. The less developed countries (LDC) aggregate is composed of China, India, and the UAR, which account for 60.5 percent of Soviet trade with less developed social and non-socialist nations 1955-1968.

8. See Chapter 7, Section C, for an explanation of this discontinuity in the U.S.S.R.-LDC time trend.

9. The U.S.S.R.-U.S.S.R. Leontief Statistic should equal 1.000 because in trade with itself the underlying capital-labor availabilities ratio, which in Heckscher-Ohlin theory determines embodied factor proportions, is the same for both trading partners.

10. Note that for regression purposes it is misleading to employ these variables as originally scaled because the neutrality or conventional zero points represent different initial values.

11. Our test of the Heckscher-Ohlin theorem I consistency of Soviet Leontief Statistics assumes that factor proportions will reflect Heckscher-Ohlin laws in bilateral exchange. Baldwin proves that bilateral Leontief Statistics need not reflect the influence of underlying factor availabilities for the overall Leontief Statistic to be Heckscher-Ohlin consistent. See Baldwin, "The Determinants of the Commodity Structure of U.S. Trade," AER, March 1971, pp. 143-44. Therefore, our demonstration that Soviet Leontief Statistics are indeed bilaterally Heckscher-Ohlin consistent is all the more interesting.

12. The linear specification alternative discussed in Section E can be tested by substituting Equation 4.9 into a linear form of Equation 4.4. Taking logs of both sides and employing unrescaled values of Ω and Y/L we obtain an R of 0.9454, with a β coefficient of 0.56021, significant at the 0.995 level.

13. The use of per capita GNP for individual years rather than the average values for the entire period 1955-1968 was dictated by the length of time separating the initial and terminal years. However no alteration of substance occurs if average values are substituted for individual year per capita GNP statistics.

14. A semi-logarithmic regression run on these observations yields an $R = 0.9077$ with a β coefficient $= 2.7745$, significant at the 0.995 level, explaining 82 percent of the variation in the dependent variable. The double log linear form produces an R of 0.9212, with a β coefficient of 0.7405, significant at the 0.995 level. Although this is marginally better than the semi-logarithmic result it should be remembered that the scaling factor diminishes its conceptual significance. Experiments with quadrant III observations bring this out quite forcefully.

15. A semi-logarithmic regression yields an R of 0.8822, with a β coefficient of 1.40098, significant at the 0.995 level, whereas the double log linear fit gives an R of 0.8405, with a β coefficient of 0.3573, also significant at the 0.995 level.

Chapter 5
**The Role of Third Factors and the Importance
of Non-Neoclassical Factor Aggregates in the
Determination of the Structure of Soviet
Commodity Trade 1955-1968**

1. The definitions of the various types of labor are taken from Vladimir Treml, "New Soviet Interindustry Data," in RECENT SOVIET ECONOMIC PERFORMANCE: SELECTED ASPECTS, RAC-P-38, August 1968, p. 35.

2. The Leontief Paradox refers to the fact that the United States demonstrates a labor intensive export bias in its trade with the rest of the world, when it is generally assumed that since America is the country with the most abundant supply of capital relative to labor, it should evidence a strong capital intensive export bias. See Wassily Leontief, "Factor Proportions and the Structure of American Trade: Further Theoretical and Empirical Analysis," REVIEW OF ECONOMICS AND STATISTICS, November 1956, 38, 386-407.

3. Jaroslav Vanek, THE NATURAL RESOURCE CONTENT OF UNITED STATES FOREIGN TRADE, 1870-1955, pp. 132-135.

4. William Travis, THE THEORY OF TRADE AND PROTECTION, pp. 94-99, and Jaroslav Vanek, "The Factor Proportions Theory: The N-Factor Case," KYKLOS, Oct. 1968, 21, 749-56.

5. The third factor notion implies that a major proportion of the value of natural resources is attributable to its scarcity rent value, rather than to labor or capital value added. If the mining industries are inefficient in the Soviet Union, as is sometimes suggested, much or all of this rent may be dissipated on the excessive cost of other factor inputs, in which case the justification for viewing natural resources as a third factor would be mitigated.

If we broaden our definition of natural resources to cover the following sectors: ferrous metallurgy (2), nonferrous metallurgy (4), industrial metal products (7), other branches of material production (66), refined petroleum (10), electricity (15), food (59), and agriculture (62) so as to include all categories that could potentially be subsumed under the natural resources rubric, the results obtained above should not be seriously affected because of the offsetting impacts of agricultural products on the one hand, and the metals and fuel groups on the other. In my opinion, however, no useful function is served by classifying natural resources in such an extremely heterogeneous manner. The decision criteria used in the classification of sectors in this study stress three characteristics: the production process, the product function, and value added. On these grounds agriculture was classified separately and is analyzed in Appendix C, while fuels and metals were deemed to fall into their own distinctive categories. Furthermore, and perhaps most importantly, it should be remembered that the theoretical justification for treating natural resources separately is that they basically constitute a third, unproduced factor. The inclusion of refined petroleum products and metallurgy with their heavy capital requirements of sophisticated technological specification I feel is not consonant with the spirit of the third factor hypothesis, and should therefore be excluded from the natural resource category. Nonetheless for completeness' sake, I have computed the effect of including these two categories for U.S.S.R.-WORLD trade. The results are broadly consonant with those presented in Table 5-1 exhibiting a further intensification of the trend shown in Figure 5-1. The only special effect worth mentioning is the fact that the labor intensity of the export bias is increased for 1955, causing the corresponding observation in Figure 5-1 to shift upwards above the value generated when all 66 sectors are included in the Leontief Statistic computation.

6. For example, see Stanislaw Wasowski, "East-West Trade and the Pattern of World Trade," in EAST WEST TRADE AND THE TECHNOLOGY GAP, pp. 171-90.

7. See Table 4-5 and Chapter 4, Section F, for a discussion of this issue.

8. See Table 4-5.

9. A regression run on the double log linear form produced an R of 0.9431, with a β coefficient of 0.63447, significant at the 0.995 level.

10. See Raymond Vernon, "International Investment and International Trade in the Product Cycle," QUARTERLY JOURNAL OF ECONOMICS, May 1966, 80, 190-207.

11. See Wassily Leontief, "Factor Proportions and the Structure of American Trade: Further Theoretical and Empirical Analysis," REVIEW OF ECONOMICS AND STATISTICS, Nov. 1956, 38, 386-407. Peter Kenen, "Skills, Human Capital and Comparative Advantage," UNIV.-NAT. BUREAU COMMITTEE ON ECONOMIC RESOURCES, CONFERENCE ON HUMAN RESOURCES, Madison, Wisconsin, November 16, 1968. Bharadwaj and Bhagwati, "Human Capital and the Pattern of Foreign Trade: The Indian Case," INDIAN ECONOMIC REVIEW, October 1967, 2, 117-42. Roskamp and McMeekin, "Factor Proportions, Human Capital and Foreign Trade: The Case of West Germany Reconsidered," QUARTERLY JOURNAL OF ECONOMICS, February 1968, 82, 152-60.

12. Michael Boretsky presents evidence confirming this position in "Comparative Progress in Technology, Productivity, and Economic Efficiency: U.S.S.R. Versus U.S.A.," NEW DIRECTIONS IN THE SOVIET ECONOMY, JEC, 1966, pp. 133-256.

13. For a more detailed evaluation of this issue see Part III.

Chapter 6
A Comparison of U.S. and U.S.S.R. Factor
Proportions and Their Consistency with the
Principles of Heckscher-Ohlin Theorem I

1. Not surprisingly semi-logarithmic and double log linear regressions run on these variables reveal no significant correlation.

2. Baldwin defines natural resources as agricultural and mining sectors (1-10); tobacco manufactures (15); lumber and wood products (20), petroleum refining (31) and primary non-ferrous metals manufactures. This list differs in important respects from the one used in our study of Soviet factor proportions, where natural resources were defined as ferrous ores (1), nonferrous ores (3), coal (8), crude petroleum (9), natural gas (11) and unprocessed timber products (51a). Baldwin's classification diverges from ours in two basic ways. First he includes natural resource processing industries such as petroleum refining and

nonferrous metallurgy. Second he includes agriculture. I have argued elsewhere that inclusion of the refined petroleum and metallurgical industries is inconsistent with the third factor hypothesis (see Chapter 5, note 6). However, an analysis of Soviet direct-plus-indirect factor ratios in these industries, coupled with an investigation of the direction of the relevant net commodity flows reveals that the trends already elaborated in our study would merely be intensified, and not altered in any fundamental way. The case for agriculture is still less compelling, especially when the effect of deleting the agricultural vector is computed in an independent calculation anyway. In the American case, Baldwin's results presented in Table 1 demonstrate that agriculture and natural resources exert opposing influences on the U.S.-WORLD Leontief Statistic. If this relationship holds for the subgroups as well, although clearly it need not, the American measure of factor proportions constitutes an underestimate of the pure nonagricultural impact of natural resources. However, since Baldwin's definition of natural resources includes more relatively capital intensive activities than our Soviet definition, the offsetting effect of the inclusion of agricultural, and natural resource related processing industries should tend to make the overall effect of deleting the natural resource sectors from the computation of the Leontief Statistic commensurable in both American and Soviet cases. In any event, the reader in comparing American and Soviet factor proportions with the influence of natural resources expunged, should be aware of the underlying definitional differences.

3. Baldwin, op. cit.

4. See note 2 for details.

5. Ibid., pp. 142-43.

6. Ibid., pp. 136, 138n., and 140. Baldwin's second skilled labor-technology definition appears under the heading "Proportion of Engineers and Scientists" in Table 4, p. 140.

For the comparable Soviet figures, see Treml, "New Soviet Interindustry Data," in RECENT SOVIET ECONOMIC PERFORMANCE: SELECTED ASPECTS, RAC-P-38, August 1968, p. 35.

Chapter 7
The Relationship Between Commodity Flow and Factor Proportion Trends in Soviet Bilateral Trade

1. For a discussion of the impact of agriculture on the structure of Soviet Leontief Statistic values see Appendix C.

2. The sectoral composition of these four categories is:

Agriculture—sector 62
Natural resources—sectors 1, 2, 3, 4, 8, 9, 10, 51a

Light industry—sectors 56, 57, 58, 59 plus the average value of 51b, 52, 54, 55, and 60

Heavy industry—sectors, 5, 6, 16-50, 53

Aggregate direct-plus-indirect factor values were computed as an unweighted average of the principal trade component factor magnitudes. Since we are not testing the third factor hypothesis, I have chosen to include refined petroleum and metallurgy into the natural resource aggregation.

The exact direct-plus-indirect factor breakdown is shown in the table below.

Table 7-1n
Aggregated Factor Input Values

Sector	Direct-Plus-Indirect Factor Inputs	
	Capital[a]	Labor[b]
Agriculture	2.117	13.996
Natural Resources	3.174	4.278
Light Industry	1.831	9.272
Heavy Industry	3.054	6.941

[a]Capital is measured in rubles of fixed capital stock per ruble of sectoral output.

[b]Labor is measured in man years per 10,000 rubles of sectoral output.

3. Disregarding some distortion due to the inexact method of aggregating direct-plus-indirect factor inputs, the difference between the Leontief Statistics computed on a 66 and a four category basis can be taken as an index of the effect particular sectoral input requirements have on the determination of factor proportion values in the Soviet context.

4. For a discussion of normalized Soviet Leontief Statistics see Chapter 4, Section E. Normalized values are used in the regression in order to avoid the semblance of a good fit due to the artificial suppression of variance necessarily entailed when an inverse numeric scale for Leontief values less than one is utilized.

5. Note, however, that Soviet heavy industrial imports from the CMEA and WEST constitute a very large portion of total imports, in sharp contrast to the negligible share of heavy industrial goods in U.S.S.R.-LDC exchange, which incidentally largely explains the difference in magnitude between Leontief Statistic values generated in Soviet trade with developed and less developed countries.

Chapter 8
False Prices, Comparative Advantage and
The Factor Proportions Structure of Soviet
International Trade

1. See Bent Hansen, A SURVEY OF GENERAL EQUILIBRIUM SYS-TEMS, (New York: 1970), pp. 14-17.

2. Morris Bornstein, "The Soviet Price System," AER, 52, 1 (March 1962).

3. See G. Smirnov's views on this subject in Holzman, "The Ruble Exchange Rate and Soviet Foreign Trade," AER, December 1968, p. 821.

Chapter 9
Conclusion

1. Janos Kornai, ANTI-EQUILIBRIUM, (Amsterdam, North Holland, 1972).

Appendix A
A Consistent International Comparison of
National Income in 15 Countries Valued
in 1967 Dollars and Computed On a
Purchasing Power Parity Basis

1. Milton Gilbert and associates, COMPARATIVE NATIONAL PRODUCTS AND PRICE LEVELS (Paris, 1958), Tables 2 and 4, pp. 23 and 28.

2. Edwin Jones, "The Emerging Pattern of Chinese Economic Revolution," in AN ECONOMIC PROFILE OF MAINLAND CHINA, JEC, 1968, p. 96.

3. Thad Alton, "Economic Structure and Growth in Eastern Europe," ECONOMIC DEVELOPMENTS IN THE COUNTRIES OF EASTERN EUROPE, JEC, 1970.

4. See Maurice Ernst, "Postwar Economic Growth in Eastern Europe," NEW DIRECTIONS IN THE SOVIET ECONOMY, JEC, 1966, pp. 911-12.

5. Paul Myers, "Demographic Trends in Eastern Europe," ECONOMIC DEVELOPMENT IN COUNTRIES OF EASTERN EUROPE, JEC, 1970, pp. 123-36.

6. Bergson, "The Comparative National Income of the USSR and USA," Conference on Research in Income and Wealth, Toronto, 1970, pp. 4-5.

7. Stanley Cohn, "Recent Trends in the Soviet Economy," ECONOMIC PERFORMANCE AND THE SOVIET MILITARY BURDEN, JEC, 1970, p. 17.

8. Murray Feshbach, "Population," in ECONOMIC PERFORMANCE AND THE SOVIET MILITARY BURDEN, JEC, 1970, p. 63.

Appendix B
Bilateral Commodity Balances and
Sectoral Factor Proportions

1. This hypothesis was unwittingly first put forward by Baldwin. See Baldwin, "Determinants of the Commodity Structure of U.S. Trade," AER, March 1971, p. 137.

2. Ibid.

Appendix C
Soviet Leontief Statistics with the
Influence of Agriculture Removed

1. Robert Baldwin, "Determinants of the Commodity Structure of U.S. Trade," AER, March 1971, p. 134.

Bibliography

Bibliography
(Cited Works)

Alton, Thad. "Economic Structure and Growth in Eastern Europe." ECO-
NOMIC DEVELOPMENTS IN COUNTRIES OF EASTERN EUROPE, JEC,
1970, pp. 41-67.

Baldwin, Robert. "Determinants of the Commodity Structure of U.S. Trade."
AER, March 1971, pp. 126-46.

Bergson, Abram. "The Comparative National Income of the USSR and USSA,"
Conference on Research in Income and Wealth, Toronto, 1970. Unpublished.

_____. THE REAL NATIONAL INCOME OF SOVIET RUSSIA SINCE
1928. Cambridge: Harvard University Press, 1961.

Bharadwaj and Bhagwati. "Human Capital and the Pattern of Foreign Trade:
The Indian Case." INDIAN ECONOMIC REVIEW, October 1967, 2, 117-42.

Bogomolov, O. "Mirovaia ekonomika i mezhdunarodniya otnoshenia."
VOPROSY EKONOMIKI, 5, (1966), pp. 15-27.

Boretsky, Michael. "Comparative Progress in Technology, Productivity, and
Economic Efficiency: U.S.S.R. Versus U.S.A." NEW DIRECTIONS IN THE
SOVIET ECONOMY, JEC, 1966, pp. 133-256.

Cohn, Stanley. "Recent Trends in the Soviet Economy." ECONOMIC PER-
FORMANCE AND THE SOVIET MILITARY BURDEN, JEC, 1970, pp.
9-17.

ECONOMIC INTEGRATION AND INDUSTRIAL SPECIALIZATION AMONG
THE MEMBERS COUNTRIES OF THE COUNCIL FOR MUTUAL ECO-
NOMIC ASSISTANCE. New York: United Nations, 1966.

Efimov, A., and L. Berri (eds.). METODY PLANEROVANIIA MEZHOTRAS-
LEVYIKH PROPORTSII, Moskva, 1967.

Eidel'man, M.P. MEZHOTRASLEVOI BALANS OBSHCHESTVENNOGO
PRODUKTA, Moskva, 1966.

Ernst, Maurice. "Postwar Economic Growth in Eastern Europe." NEW DIREC-
TIONS IN THE SOVIET ECONOMY, JEC, 1966, pp. 873-916.

Feshback, Murray. "Population." ECONOMIC PERFORMANCE AND THE
SOVIET MILITARY BURDEN, JFC, 1970, pp. 60-70.

Gallik, Daniel. THE SOVIET FINANCIAL SYSTEM. Washington, D.C.: U.S.
Department of Commerce, 1968.

Haberler, Gottfried. A SURVEY OF INTERNATIONAL TRADE THEORY.
Princeton, 1965.

Hirschman, Albert O. NATIONAL POWER AND THE STRUCTURE OF
FOREIGN TRADE. Berkeley: University of California, 1945.

Holzman, Franklin D. "Foreign Trade" in Bergson and Kuznets (eds.). ECO-
NOMIC TRENDS IN THE SOVIET UNION. Cambridge: Harvard University
Press, 1963, pp. 283-332.

Iasin, E. and M. Fidler. VESTNIK STATISTIKI, Moscow, 12, 1965, pp. 36-43.

Jones, Edwin. "The Emerging Pattern of Chinese Economic Revolution." AN ECONOMIC PROFILE OF MAINLAND CHINA, JEC, 1968, pp. 77-96.

Kaser, Michael. COMECON: INTEGRATION PROBLEMS OF PLANNED ECONOMIES. London: Oxford, 1967.

Kenen, Peter. "Skills, Human Capital and Comparative Advantage." UNIV.-NAT. BUREAU COMMITTEE ON ECONOMIC RESOURCES' CONFERENCE ON HUMAN RESOURCES, Madison, Wisconsin, November 16, 1968.

Kornai, Janos. ANTI-EQUILIBRIUM. Amsterdam: North Holland, 1972.

Kuznets, Simon. MODERN ECONOMIC GROWTH. New Haven: Yale University Press, 1969.

Leontief, Wassily. "Domestic Production and Foreign Trade: The American Capital Position Re-examined." PROCEEDINGS OF THE AMERICAN PHILOSOPHICAL SOCIETY, September 1953, 332-49.

_____. "Factor Proportions and the Structure of American Trade: Further Theoretical and Empirical Analysis." REVIEW OF ECONOMICS AND STATISTICS, November 1956, pp. 386-407.

Michaely, Michael. CONCENTRATION IN INTERNATIONAL TRADE. Amsterdam: North-Holland Publishing Company, 1967.

Montias, John. ECONOMIC DEVELOPMENT IN COMMUNIST RUMANIA. Cambridge: M.I.T., 1968.

Myers, Paul. "Demographic Trends in Eastern Europe." ECONOMIC DEVELOPMENTS IN THE COUNTRIES OF EASTERN EUROPE, JEC, 1970, pp. 68-148.

NARODNOYE KHOZYAISTVO SSSR V 1965, AND 1968G. Moscow, 1966, 1969.

NATIONAL ACCOUNTS OF LESS DEVELOPED COUNTRIES, 1950-1966. O.E.C.D., Geneva, 1968.

NATIONAL ACCOUNTS OF OECD COUNTRIES, 1950-1968, O.E.C.D., Geneva, 1970.

Pryor, Frederick. THE COMMUNIST FOREIGN TRADE SYSTEM. Cambridge: M.I.T., 1963.

Roskamp and McMeekin. "Factor Proportions, Human Capital and Foreign Trade: The Case of West Germany Reconsidered." QJE, February 1968, 82, 152-60.

Samuelson, Paul. "International Trade and the Equalization of Factor Prices." ECONOMIC JOURNAL, June 1948, pp. 163-84.

_____. "International Factor-Price Equilization Once Again." ECONOMIC JOURNAL, June 1949, pp. 181-97.

Thornton, Judith. "Differential Capital Charges and Resource Allocation in Soviet Industry." JOURNAL OF POLITICAL ECONOMY, May 1971, pp. 545-77.

Travis, William. THE THEORY OF TRADE AND PROTECTION. Cambridge: Harvard, 1964.

Treml, Vladimir G. INPUT-OUTPUT ANALYSIS AND SOVIET PLANNING. Unpublished, 1964.

———. "New Soviet Capital Data." SOVIET STUDIES, 18, 3 (January 1967): 290-95.

———. "New Soviet Inter-Industry Data." SOVIET ECONOMIC PERFORMANCE: 1966-67, JEC, pp. 146-47.

———. "New Soviet Interindustry Data." RECENT SOVIET ECONOMIC PERFORMANCE: SELECTED ASPECTS. Research Analysis Corporation, RAC-P-38, August 1968.

———. "The 1959 Soviet Input-Output Table" in NEW DIRECTIONS IN THE SOVIET ECONOMY, JEC, 1966, pp. 257-70.

———. THE 1959 SOVIET INTERSECTORAL FLOW TABLE. Volume I, Research Analysis Corporation, Technical Paper RAC-TP-137, November 1964.

Vanek, Jaroslav. "The Factor Proportions Theory: The N-Factor Case." KYKLOS, Oct. 1968, 21, 749-56.

———. THE NATURAL RESOURCE CONTENT OF UNITED STATES FOREIGN TRADE, 1870-1955. Cambridge: Harvard, 1963.

Vernon, Raymond. "International Investment and International Trade in the Product Cycle." QJE, May 1966, 80, 190-207.

VNESHNIAIA TORGOVLIA SSSR, STATISTICHESKII SBORNIK, 1918-1966, Moskva, 1968.

VNESHNIAIA TORGOVLIA SSSR ZA 1968, Moskva, 1969.

Wasowski, Stanislaw. "East-West Trade and the Pattern of World Trade." EAST WEST TRADE AND THE TECHNOLOGY GAP, New York: Praeger, 1970, pp. 171-90.

Wilczynski, Josef. THE ECONOMICS AND POLITICS OF EAST-WEST TRADE. New York: Praeger, 1969.

Wiles, Peter. COMMUNIST INTERNATIONAL ECONOMICS. New York: Praeger, 1969.

Wu, Yuan-Li. THE ECONOMY OF COMMUNIST CHINA. New York: Praeger, 1965.

YEAR BOOK OF NATIONAL ACCOUNT STATISTICS, 1969, VOLUME II, INTERNATIONAL TABLES. New York: United Nations, 1970.

Index

Index

About the Author

Steven S. Rosefielde, an Assistant Professor of Economics at the University of North Carolina, Chapel Hill was born in Brooklyn, New York, August 1942. Long interested in economic, historical and political problems of socialism in general and Soviet socialism in particular, he pursued these interests consecutively at Ohio Wesleyan, The London School of Economics and Harvard University. At the London School of Economics he was tutored in Soviet Government by Leonard Schapiro, and Soviet Economics by Alec Nove and Alfred Zauberman. Professor Rosefielde holds the B.A. in history and philosophy from Ohio Wesleyan, the M.A. degree in Soviet Regional Studies and the Ph.D. in Economics both from Harvard, where he studied under the supervision of Professors Abram Bergson, Alexander Gerschenkron and Anne Carter. At the moment he is actively pursuing his Soviet input-output research in conjunction with Professor Vladimir Treml, aided by a joint Duke-UNC Ford Foundation sponsored grant.